CHRONICLES OF
AUNT HILMA

Chronicles
of
Aunt Hilma

AND OTHER EAST HILLSIDE SWEDES

Michael Fedo

North Star Press of St. Cloud, Inc.

Design: Corinne Dwyer
Cover art and illustrations: Judy Fedo

ISBN: 0-87839-068-5

All rights reserved. Printed in the United States of America by Versa Press of East Peoria, Illinois.

Published by:

North Star Press of St. Cloud, Inc.
P.O. Box 451
St. Cloud, Minnesota 56302

With love,
for Judy,
who insisted I write these stories.

Contents

Preface

Several years ago at the annual lutefisk and meatball supper at a local Lutheran church, a couple brought their three-year-old son to his first lutefisk feed. The lad, a fourth generation American of Swedish descent, was dressed in a tidy dark suit with a red tie. His hair had been freshly slicked down and parted. A quiet, somber little fellow, he sat at the long table among adults who dropped substantial servings of lutefisk (codfish purposefully destroyed by a bath in a vat of lye, then dried to the consistency of a wood plank, and boiled until it turns into a transluscent bluish-white fish jello) onto their plates and carried on animated conversations. The youngster carefully sampled the lime jello salad containing shredded carrots and slices of canned peaches, the store-bought crescent rolls, and the boiled potatoes, before his spoon probed a small bit of the evening's *piece de résistance*—lutefisk—which the unsuspecting little guy brought to his lips. He tasted briefly, then cried out, "Mom, it's poop!"

Though many claim that lutefisk is a culinary manifestation of dementia, it is a subject of uniquely Scandinavian drollery. Even the most chauvinistic Swede or Norwegian can relate to the story of the three-year-old's initial encounter with lutefisk. I suspect that experience was not so different from their own.

Notwithstanding, the ritual of eating this so-called comestible, is so inculcated into the souls of Scandinavian Americans as to form a basis for defining their characters.

Most non-appreciators of lutefisk are doubtless amused to learn that each year Scandinavians assemble in church basements to celebrate their ethnicity by eating lutefisk. And they are forced to wonder, what sort of person would deem the bizarre preparation of this fish suitable for human consumption?

It's true that most Americans of Swedish and Norwegian descent do indeed smack their lips over platters of the slippery, quivering cod, and probably because they do, they develop other crotchets indigenous to those who eat lutefisk. Some of those crotchets are chronicled here, especially as they relate to my great Aunt Hilma Norquist and some of the other Swedish-Americans who populated the East Hillside neighborhood in Duluth, where I grew up.

While I was raised among such people, I also hold something of an outsider's perspective, being Italian on my father's side. Swedish relatives and neighbor's eccentricities delighted me, though these people would never have regarded themselves as humorous. But their responses to the rhythms of daily life amused me, and, largely because of them, I enjoyed a cheerful childhood.

I have tried to capture the mood and spirit of those people and those days on these pages, recounting as best I can, what life was like with these long-departed men and women who ate and enjoyed lutefisk, and who figured so prominently in my formative years.

CHRONICLES OF
AUNT HILMA

1

The Roomer

Throughout my childhood during the 1940s and 1950s my family—Mom, Dad, younger brother, David, and later, youngest brother, Stephen—lived in a two-story, white house on Tenth Avenue East and Tenth Street in Duluth, Minnesota. Occupying the house next door on our north side, was my maternal grandmother, Augusta Norquist, her unmarried daughter Ada, and Hilma Norquist, Grandma's sixtyish, spinster sister-in-law.

The homes, which had been built by Mom's father, Eric, were virtually identical. Each featured an enclosed front porch—an extended drawing room at Grandma's house, but a repository for bicycles, camping gear and athletic paraphernalia at our house.

The houses shared a common driveway, which separated them, and a single-car, wood garage. None of the Norquist women drove, however, so for all intents and purposes, it was our garage. The only Norquist who ever parked in the driveway was Mom's older brother, Howard, who invariably left his car there at the precise moment Dad had to hurry out to a meeting or a rehearsal for the Duluth Symphony, of which he was a charter member. While I'm probably exaggerating somewhat here, I also recall that whenever Howard parked in the driveway and Dad had to dash off somewhere, Howard's car refused to start. Howard would always tell Dad that as far as he was concerned, our driveway was a jinx on his car, that it never gave him a speck of trouble anywhere else, but would always shut down when he parked in the driveway. He just couldn't understand it, he always said. Just as regularly, Dad would say that he didn't care if Howard understood it or not, and he should park his damn jalopy in the street from then on. And maybe the next time Howard visited, he would. But the car never failed to start when parked in the street, and sure enough, subsequent visits found Howard's old Chevy stuck in the driveway again.

The business of Howard's car parked in our driveway formed the foundation of Dad's relationship with his brother-in-law, though he never said anything to Grandma for fear of hurting her feelings, nor to Hilma, who often found Howard's antics irritating. And Dad's complaining about Howard would only give Hilma more fodder to use when ragging on poor Grandma, as gentle and sweet-natured a soul as God breathed life into.

Throughout the 1940s, Grandma used to rent out the spare upstairs bedroom of her house to students, salesmen, or itinerant laborers. At times the room was vacant for weeks on end, since prospective roomers had to pass modest muster imposed by Grandma, who merely insisted that no liquor be brought into the premises, and there be no smoking, except in the rented room with the door closed.

Getting past Aunt Hilma's requirement was another matter. Though Grandma owned the house, Hilma retained certain rights, as she had forsaken a career and marriage to care for my grandfather's aged and dying parents. Grandfather, before he died, had made it clear that Hilma was to always have a home with his family because of her selflessness.

A severe woman with firmly set mouth, Hilma's brown-gray hair was always tied back in a bun. She wore black linen dresses and a green wool sweater summer and winter. Hilma not only was opposed to smoking and drinking, but to frivolous laughter and members of the Lutheran church. She occasionally exercised power in nixing potential roomers. They may have dressed shabbily, or expressed no interest in attending church. She turned down one man for being Lutheran. "Da Lutrans make a big show of church on Sundays, but da rest of da veek, vatch out." Hilma, who was the only member of her Swedish clan born in America, nonetheless had the thickest Scandinavian accent of her surviving sisters.

Now and again while Hilma happened to be downtown or at Garon's Mill in West Duluth, where she worked as a seamstress, Grandma would accept a man without Hilma's approval. Then Hilma would sulk and keep to her room for several days, emerging only to eat well after Grandma and Ada had eaten.

In time, however, she'd come to accept the new roomer, if he caused no trouble. This did not mean she would speak to him, and, in fact, she never to my recollection, spoke directly to a roomer. If she had a complaint, as she often did: "Da roomer used up all da hot vater," or "Da roomer left his door open and I seen some filty magazines on his bed"—my peace-loving grandmother tried to soothe her. If unsatisfied with Grandma's efforts, Hilma would approach my father to deal with the malefactor.

Dad always asked what Hilma would have him say to the roomer, which incensed her. "Vat do yew tink yew should say?" she'd ask crossly. "Uff. If I vas a man, I'd see tew it he got plenty of trouble."

And Dad would agree to at least talk to the man.

I remember when a roomer named Edward was leaving,

and gave Grandma two weeks' notice. She placed a small ad in the newspaper and waited for responses. There were none, and she anticipated a lengthy wait before filling the room. Rarely dismayed at this prospect, for it had happened before, this time she wanted to send twenty-five dollars to the Baptist church to kick off the new building fund. The money would be available only if the room were rented.

Edward, learning of the difficulty Grandma was having in replacing him, told her of an acquaintance at work who might be looking for a new place. Edward said he'd talk to the fellow and have him stop by for an interview.

Edward had been tolerated rather well by Hilma, as he was not a mirthful man. In his late twenties, he wore dark horn-rimmed glasses, and was memorable only for his prodigious appetite. The only meal he took at Grandma's was breakfast, which never varied. It consisted of an entire box of cold cereal emptied into a large mixing bowl and topped with most of a quart of milk.

Edward's acquaintance was named Stiles—I never caught his first name. He arrived with his gear on a Saturday morning, shortly after Hilma had boarded a bus for downtown. Grandma may have been uneasy about taking him, but Stiles told her he had no place else to go and was counting on getting that room. He apologized for not being able to pay more than a week in advance, but he was steadily employed, and said he understood the house rules. He would be no bother.

With some hesitation, Grandma took him to the room and let him bounce a time or two on the bed. He checked the closet and said he'd take the room. Then he handed Grandma seven one-dollar bills, and left to attend some errands.

Hilma returned about noon, and Grandma told her about the new roomer. Hilma was skeptical, reminding Grandma that the last time Grandma had accepted a roomer without her consent, the bounder had left town owing two weeks' rent.

About three o'clock, Stiles returned, said nothing and

went upstairs.

Perhaps an hour later, Hilma went to her room for a sweater, only to find Stiles in her bed. She was mortified, for not only was a stranger beneath her covers, but she discovered he'd also failed to negotiate his way to the bathroom down the hall. He had thrown up on her lampstand.

Hilma stomped downstairs, angry tears spurting from her eyes. "Gustie," she snapped in a hoarse whisper. "Da new man is drunk in my bed. He womited, and da room stinks."

Grandma slowly wiped her hands on her white apron. "Are you sure, Hilma? Maybe the poor fellow's sick."

"He's drunk," Hilma snarled. "Trew up in my room. I'm yust sick about it. How are ve going to get him out of dere, Gustie?"

"Mike will talk to him," Grandma said. She turned to me. I was in her kitchen, downing my fourth ginger cookie. "Mickey, will you bring your daddy over here right away? Tell him we've got a little trouble with the new roomer."

"Tell him ve got *lots* of trouble," Hilma harrumphed. "Oooh, I'm so mad I could yust spit."

I bounded across the twelve-foot driveway. Dad was in the basement working on the washing machine. "Grandma says they got trouble with the roomer," I said.

Dad grimaced. "What's up?" He wiped his hands on a chamois cloth.

"I think he's drunk and threw up in Hilma's room."

Dad let a long sigh escape his lips. He started up the stairs and crossed the driveway with me at his heels.

"Mike, he's stinking drunk," cried Hilma as we stepped into the front porch. The summer sun had heated it to more than ninety degrees. My father, already perspiring from his efforts to wrench an ill-tempered motor from our washer, sought the comfort of Grandma's shaded parlor to hear her story.

But Hilma already had her bony, arthritic fingers clamped around his wrist. "Yew've yust got to get him to leaf, Mike. He's in *my* bed." She clutched Dad at both elbows as he entered the house. "Ewen if he says he'll pay a hundred dollars, ve von't haf him." She tried to usher Dad up the stairs.

Dad eased free of her grasp and approached Grandma. "I'll see what I can do," he said, and Grandma shook her head.

"He could be ill, Mike," she offered.

"He's drunk," came Hilma's protest from the first landing.

Dad sighed again. "Stay here," he told me, and ascended the stairs. I could hear only muffled voices from my vantage point below, owing to Hilma's angry expositions to Grandma.

Several minutes later, Dad came down. "He'll be gone soon. You gotta be careful about who you let in your house, Grandma."

"Dat's vat I say," Hilma adamantly affirmed. "Yew can say dat again." She blew into her lace hankie.

"Won't you stay for some coffee, Mike?" Grandma asked.

"No, I don't think so."

"Who can tink of coffee at a time like dis?" Hilma muttered hotly. "Yew're yust lucky, Gustie, it vasn't yewr room got all messed up. Den yew wouldn't be tinking about no coffee."

"Shush, Hilma," Grandma said softly. "Everything will be all right."

"Dat's vat yew tink," Hilma said.

There was some clamoring at the top of the staircase and Stiles descended, struggling with a seaman's duffel bag. Rumpled and red-faced, he looked at no one, thus escaping Hilma's withering glare. No one moved to help him with the door, and he cursed softly as he managed to get it open before barging out into the late afternoon. He hoisted the bag to his shoulder, hawked and spit into Tenth Avenue, and started unevenly down the hill.

"Thanks a million, Mike," Grandma said. "You sure you won't have coffee?"

Dad again declined.

"Mike," Hilma started, "yew should of tot tew have him clean up dat mess. I tell yew, I'm as mad as a hen." She grabbed a dishpan and cloth and started up the stairs. "Dat's da last vun, Gustie. No more roomers." She went up and seconds later wailed, "oh, noo-ooo."

Dad, from the foot of the stairs, called, "What's wrong, Hilma?"

"Da dirty skunk vet my bed tew," she sobbed angrily and slammed her door.

Dad threw me a faintly amused glance, and we hurried upstairs to aid Hilma. We found my great aunt ripping bedding from the mattress and, with remarkable strength for a woman so frail in appearance, removed the mattress from the spring and shoved it out the front bedroom window, where it rested on the roof of the porch. Composing herself then, she went back downstairs.

All the excitement made me hungry, and I prevailed upon Grandma for more cookies and milk. Dad went home to finish with the washing machine. Hilma took the chair opposite me and didn't speak.

Finally Grandma said, "You know, he paid for the whole week. You don't suppose we should try to give him back his money, do you?"

A gutteral eruption escaped from Hilma's throat, and she gripped the sides of the kitchen table. "Yew're nuts, Gustie."

"I'm sure he didn't mean no harm," Grandma said.

"No harm? No harm? Womit and pee, yew call dat no harm?" She sat back, her breaths came in labored gasps. She stood up and turned to face my grandmother. "Don't expect me to peel no potatoes or wash no dishes tonight, Gustie," she said evenly. "I've had enough for vun day."

I left the house then and started back across the driveway to our house. Uncle Howard had just pulled into the drive and was standing by his 1937 Chevy. The hood was up and great clouds of steam were billowing out of his radiator.

He stepped away from the car when he saw me. "Well, Mickey," he said, squinting. "I don't suppose anything exciting has been going on with Mother and Auntie. Wasn't even going to drop in today, but I was in the neighborhood when this durned old buggy started acting up. Listen, don't say nothing to your dad, okay? Shoot, she'll start up fine once she cools down a tad."

Later that evening, when Dad was in his usual hurry to get to the symphony concert at the Armory, he got grease smudges on his tux from having to help Howard push the Chevy out of the driveway.

2

Amos Vachter,
Actor Extraordinaire

Vaudeville had largely disappeared from the American landscape by the time I came along, having been replaced by radio and talking motion pictures. It survived into the 1940s, by playing backwater river towns and remote rural regions of the country. Aunt Hilma, though, cared not a whit that an art form was dying before her very eyes. Her austere Baptist upbringing forbade her ever darkening the door of a theater—vaudeville or movie. Nor was she in the least bit interested in attending any sort of show, remarking that shows were a waste of time and portrayed alcohol and to-bacco as glamorous. She used to sum up her reaction to shows with one word: "Ish."

Thus, I certainly wasn't surprised that she registered great disgust when Aunt Winnie, who ran a boarding house near the site of the old family farm in Deerwood, Minnesota, boarded an actor and a few crew men from a touring troupe slated to play two evenings in town. As it happened, Hilma was visiting Aunt Winnie at the time and had brought me

9

along with her.

We hadn't been inside Aunt Winnie's huge old house thirty minutes when Hilma noticed the actor, who entered, offered a courtly bow to Winnie, and "Good day to you," then headed up the stairs, singing "Here we go loop de loo; Here we go loop de lai," rather more loudly than Hilma deemed appropriate. He was also festooned with a purple paisley ascot and a white Stetson, a pearl cigarette holder clamped between his teeth. His voice, rich, sonorous, orotund—was not the voice associated with the ordinary farmhands or drifters who usually roomed with Winnie.

"Vat in da vorld?" Hilma gasped, hurrying to the staircase and following the man up with her gaze. "Is he drunk, or vat?"

"Oh, no, nuting like dat, Hilma," said Aunt Winnie, removing a pan of biscuits from the oven. Hilma's elder sister, Winnie, born in Sweden, was a stout, matronly woman with white hair piled high on her crown in a layered braid, held in place with a blue comb.

She did not resemble Hilma, for she was shorter, thicker, and broader of face. But her countenance, like Hilma's, was stern, and the corners of her mouth pulled downward, as did Hilma's, into a perpetual frown.

Winnie used a spatula to place the hot biscuits onto the brown grocery bags she had cut and flattened and spread on her kitchen table. "Yew can have vun later, Mickey," she said to me. "After dey've cooled." Then she faced Hilma who had returned to the kitchen. "Dat man is an actor, Hilma," she said. "He's vit da show dat's playing here dis evening. He's a little odd, I know, but he'll only be here a day or tew, so I guess ve can put up with dat."

"An actor vit a show?" Hilma clutched the back of a kitchen chair and leaned on it for support. "Yew let an actor vit a show stay here in yewr house, Vinnie?"

"Vy yes, Hilma. Yes, I don't see nutting wrong vit dat."

"Oh yew don't do yew? Vinnie, dose people got no morals

at all. Dey're up late at night tarryhooting all ower town and raising all kinds of dickens. Dey drink liquor tew. You don't allow no alcohol in da house, do yew?"

"No, a course not. I run a good, clean place, and I don't stand for no shenanigans needer," Winnie said, shaking her finger.

"Den yew've got to give dat man da boot, Vinnie," Hilma said. "Uddervise, he'll have da whole place in cahoots, and yew von't be able to do nutting about it."

Vinnie looked at her sister for a moment. "Phooey, Hilma," she said with a huff. "I don't believe dat stuff."

"Vinnie, yew vas raised in da Baptist church, same as me. God don't like show people, and dere sure von't be none in heaben. And if dere von't be none in heaben, dere shouldn't be none in yewr house."

Clearly taken back, Winnie stood near the table, thinking. Neither she nor Hilma had noticed the showman come back downstairs and eavesdrop in the doorway between the foyer and the kitchen.

Deftly he glided into the kitchen. "Ladies," he said, bowing again. "Do I detect dissension due perhaps to my presence?"

Hilma flushed. "Yew're an actor, ain't yew?"

"Precisely, madam, precisely," he said. "Amos Vachter's the name, and I don't believe I've had the pleasure of yours." He smiled broadly beneath a pencil-thin black mustache.

"Oh, um, dis here's my sister, Hilma Norquist from Dulut, Mr. Vachter," Vinnie said, flustered. She rested her hand on my shoulder. "And da boy is Mickey, her niece's boy. He lives right next door to Hilma, vich is real nice."

"Indeed," said Mr. Vachter, taking Hilma's hand and kissing it. She pulled it away and rubbed it with her other hand as he turned to shake hands with me. "Splendid looking young fellow," he announced. "I should be proud to have a lad like this as a son. Indeed I should." He smiled down at me.

I looked up at him. The atmosphere about Amos Vachter was redolent of bay rum.

Hilma threw her arms about my shoulders, sheltering me from Mr. Vachter. "Tank da Lord he's not yewrs," said Hilma stiffly. "He'd newer go to church, and instead yew'd teach him to carouse and take adwantage of ladies. I heard all about yew show people."

"My dear lady, you do me wrong," Mr. Vachter said. "I am, and always have considered myself an upstanding, patriotic American citizen, upholding the highest verities of our culture—namely the flag of our land and a rock-solid family—the very foundation of our civilization."

"Yew got a slippery vay of talking, mister," Hilma said warily.

"Oh, my dear Hilma. Lovely name, Hilma. My late wife's mother's name was Hilma. I bet you didn't know that, did you?"

Hilma offered an aspirate grunt, while Winnie said, "My, how nice."

Hilma swallowed. "Oh," she said, finally.

Mr. Vachter smiled again. "Ladies, I take no offense here at all. It's what you might call an occupational hazard of the profession. No one likes to be ill-thought of, Hilma. But we actors," he said, trilling the "r," "we actors, get rather used to the vilification, the fear and loathing, albeit, we'd rather not countenance such. What was it Prince Hamlet said?" He lifted his hand and touched his forehead with the tips of his fingers.

The three of us were quite thunderstruck at Mr. Vachter's theatricality, and we stood mouths agape as the man leaned against the door jam, a distant, faraway gaze in his eyes. "'Good name in man and woman, dear my lord, is the immediate jewel of their soul.'" He smiled. "Hamlet was a sage for the ages, ladies. Now," he said, striding toward me and hoisting me up in the air, "to protect my good name, you ladies and young gentleman here, would do me the distinct honor of attending our performance here this evening. You'll soon see I'm not the ogre of your initial perceptions."

"Vy dat vould be vunderful," gushed Aunt Winnie.

"Vouldn't needer," harrumphed Hilma. "It might be vunderful, Vinnie, if yew were a headen. Ve can't take little Mickey to see something like dat."

Mr. Vachter held up his hand. "I assure you, my dear Hilma, that this is a religious play, about good and stalwart men of the cloth, shall we say, and that in every instance, the hand of a loving God bathes our stage in the light of love and glory." He trilled the "r" on glory.

"Dere, yew see, Hilma. Dey have a show about ministers and eweryting. Ve should go and see. I newer been to a show."

Hilma gave the old actor the fish-eye. "Are yew sure yew ain't yust pulling our legs, mister?"

With a flourish, Mr. Vachter removed a long, thin wallet from his jacket pocket. He opened it and produced three tickets, which he handed to Hilma. "Three on the aisle," he said. Then in a confidential stage whisper, he added, "Third row. Practically the best seats in the house. And more than that, I should be so very honored if you'd pay a call in my dressing room backstage following the performance."

"Wow," I said.

"Now, I ain't said ve're going," Hilma said, hedging.

Mr. Vachter said, "The curtain is at eight o'clock sharp," then turned and started for the stairs. Before mounting them he paused and bowed. "Until then, adieu."

"Vel, I newer, Hilma," Aunt Winnie said. "I should say."

"I don't know about dis," Hilma said, looking at the tickets.

"Please, Hilma," I begged. "We can go, okay?"

"About men of da cloth," Winnie said. "Ve maybe should see vun like dat, huh, Hilma? Can't hurt nutting, far as I can see."

"Yah, but sometimes, Vinnie, yew can't see past da nose on yewr face," Hilma said. "And yew know dat's da trut."

In the end, though, Hilma relented. I think she was as curious as Aunt Winnie and I to go inside a theater tent and see a real show for the first time in our lives.

Though it was mid-summer, with its attendant humidity, the sisters put on dark Sunday-dress coats and hats. A white shirt and dark slacks had to do for me.

We were driven to what appeared to be a fairgrounds by Winnie's bachelor son, Hubert, who insisted on taking his dog Gutser in the car with us. Gutser was a large animal, at least part great dane, and the back seat of Hubert's Studebaker was his territory. Despite his size, he was not an intimidating animal. Quite the opposite. He insisted on affection, and thus gamboled about the back seat from my lap to Hilma's, slobbering drool and depositing fine tan hairs on our dark clothing.

Every few minutes Hubert would holler back at the dog, "Jeez, Louise, Gutser, settle down, willya?" And each time Hubert spoke, the animal would lie down, a full sprawl across the laps of Aunt Hilma and me. There Gutser would whimper pitifully, until unable to bear it any longer, he would bound up and lick Hilma's cheek, askewing her hat and hair, leaving more foamy dog spittle on her black coat.

Hilma's jaws were tight throughout the ten-minute drive, and she did not speak, except to utter groans of exasperation. I think she thought that if she opened her mouth, Gutser's large, pink, hyperactive tongue might find it.

Finally we arrived. Hilma and I were a mess, but dog drool is not as out of place on the clothing of an eight-year-old boy as on the finery of a sixty-year-old spinster.

"Dog, anyvay," muttered Hilma, dabbing at her coat with her fragile lace hankie. "Dog—dat—dog, anyvay. Lewk at me, Vinnie," she said, facing her sister. "Lewk vat dat dumb dog of Hubert's done to my clothes. I'm yust sick, Vinnie. I'm yust a wreck."

"Oh, now, Hilma, hush," Winnie said. "Gutser is a lively dog, dat's all, and he *liked* yew. He gets a little excited ven he's around folks he likes."

"I don't care dat he likes me," Hilma rasped hoarsely.
"But dat dumb dog half licked me to det. Lewk at me, Vinnie,
I got dog lick all ower my coat. And ewen my hair's a mess.
I can tell ve had no business coming here. It's da Lord's vay
of saying, 'Hilma, yew know yew shouldn't be here, and to
punish yew and Mickey, dat dumb dog vill be lapping yew
up and down.'"

"I tink yew lewk yust fine, Hilma," Winnie offered diplomatically.

"Sure, yew vould say dat, Vinnie. It vasn't yew in da
back seat vit dat stoopid beast." Hilma continued forcefully
but ineffectually dabbing at Gutser's drool.

Winnie gently touched Hilma's arm. "It'll be dark inside, Hilma, and no vun vill see anyting on yew."

"Besides that," I piped, "Hubert's gone and won't be
back for us until after the show. We'd have to walk all the
way back to the house."

"Dat's right," said Winnie brightly. "So Hilma, yew
might yust as vell make da best of it and enjoy yewrself."

We started toward the entrance. "I tell yew dis, Vinnie,"
Hilma said. "On da vay back, I ain't sitting vit dat dog."

The play that evening was about "men of the cloth," as
Mr. Vachter had said. The main characters were two Cath-
olic priests. No doubt Hilma would have preferred they be
Baptist ministers, but she sat stiffly, huffing and grunting
back and forth between me and Aunt Winnie about how she
had been fooled by that actor staying at Winnie's house, and
how Winnie should throw him out in the street.

However, by the end of the first act, Hilma had been
won over. There was a warm and tenderhearted quality to
the play about a young priest coming into a parish and up-
setting the comfortable status quo and routine established
by the older priest. There was also a lot of humor, and Winnie
laughed until tears ran down her cheeks. Hilma wouldn't go
that far, of course, but she did allow herself several broad

smiles.

By the end of the play, though, she too was laughing right along with the rest of the audience.

Hilma started up the aisle to leave, but Winnie tugged her back. "We're supposed to see Mr. Vachter backstage," she said.

An usher directed us to the backstage area, where Mr. Vachter sat in a cubicle with a large towel around his neck. He was smoking a cigarette and wiping greasepaint from his face with a large handful of cold cream. He turned as we came in. "Ah, my dear friends," he said, rising. "How good of you to drop in. And now I pray you won't cut me to the quick and blaspheme my performance, will you? I'd literally bleed if you do."

Aunt Winnie looked at Hilma and spoke. "Ve surely enyoyed ourselves, Mr. Wachter," she said, deliberately choosing her words. "And bote Hilma and me tot yew vere yust tops."

"Oh, thank you, dear lady," said Mr. Vachter, and he kissed Aunt Winnie's hand.

"It vas pretty good," Hilma said softly.

"Vell, ve really liked it anyvay," Aunt Winnie said, nodding.

"Ve got to go now, Vinnie," said Hilma, backing away.

"Of course you do, ladies and sonny-boy," the actor said. "I expect I'll be rather late this evening, madam." He nodded at Winnie. "I'd surely appreciate it if you'd keep the front door ajar. It takes a rather long time to clean up after a production such as this, and then we have to get things ready for our play tomorrow evening. I'd hate to have you wait up, or worse, be roused to let me in. And, oh yes, since you've enjoyed this production so, please be my guest at the performance tomorrow as well." He held three more tickets in his hand, which Winnie snatched before Hilma could protest.

"Tank yew, and good night den," Winnie said, as we left Mr. Vachter and the tent. We found Hubert's car in the lot, sans Gutser, who, Hubert said, was just too tired out to make the return trip.

I remember little of the next day, as my concentration seemed focused on attending a second show featuring Mr. Vachter's company of players. I do remember, though, Hilma's understated reactions to the previous night's play. Every once in a while, she would make some comment in the kitchen, or in the parlor where the two women sat knitting together. And Winnie always countered with, "But yew got tew admit it, Hilma, yew tot it vas pretty funny."

"Yah," Hilma would say, returning to her knitting, the needles clicking softly, the wind chimes on Winnie's porch tinkling in the summer breeze and carrying into the parlor.

Finally it was time to go once more to the tent show. Hilma and Winnie had washed my shirt and pants, but could do nothing about Hilma's coat. However, Winnie made Hubert promise not to bring Gutser this time, making the ride to the fairgrounds uneventful.

The play this night, however, was not. Titled, "Over the Hill to the Poorhouse," the story dealt with a crooked, greedy banker who fleeced his partner, murdered him, and foreclosed on his widow's home, sending her penniless to the poorhouse.

Mr. Vachter played the slick malefactor with such intensity, such obvious relish, that the audience talked of forming a lynch mob and dealing with him right there on the spot. In fact, at the end of the first act, several young farmhands rushed the stage with the clear intention of thrashing Mr. Vachter. However, the heroine stopped them. "Boys, this is only pretend," she cried. "Nobody's really hurt. And besides, he'll get his punishment in the end. You'll see."

"I certainly hope so," said Hilma hotly. She flushed then, and turned to Winnie. "I told yew dat man vas a scoundrel."

"Yes, yew did, Hilma. I should of listened tew yew."

"Ooooo, he's a piker, dat vun," Hilma affirmed. "I can yudge a man pretty good ven I see him, and I knew dat he vould be nutting but trouble. Look vat he done to dat poor voman. Took her house avay from her and yust sends her licketysplit to da poorhouse."

Even though the villain did get his comeuppance at play's end, he didn't suffer enough to suit that evening's audience. Aunt Winnie was still so upset five minutes after the curtain descended that she wept. Hilma bade her sit and wait while she took me backstage to see Mr. Vachter.

He greeted us with his customary smile. "Well, and how—?"

"Don't yew 'how' me," Hilma said, shaking her finger under his nose. "Yew do a ting like dat to a helpless old voman and I don't ewer vant to see yew again. Yew're a beast, is vat yew are."

"Oh, now, my dear Hilma," stated Mr. Vachter. "This was a play after all, and not real. Why, the lady in question is an old dear friend of mine. Everyone involved with this show is a friend of mine. We're a lovely little family here, Hilma, and you must understand that."

"I understand vat I vant to understand," she snapped. "I ain't such a fool as my sister out dere, who's crying like nobody's business. Yew do a ting like dat to Vinnie, and I say yew're a bad man." She tugged my arm, and dragged me back out front, where Winnie slowly regained her composure.

On the ride back to Winnie's house, Hilma repeated that Mr. Vachter could not spend another night in Winnie's House. As soon as we arrived, she helped Winnie pack Mr. Vachter's things in his satchel. Then Hubert carried it to the front porch. By eleven o'clock the house was locked.

A little past midnight, Mr. Vachter returned, a bit down in his cups. He banged on the door, which wakened me. "Let me in, dear friends," he hollered. "Open this damned hearth and home, I say." He hammered at the door with his fist.

Hilma, sleeping in the same room as I, got up and took her teeth from the cup near her bed. She inserted them, put on her robe and went downstairs. I followed as far as the landing, where I sat and peered down as she approached the door. "Yewr tings are right dere vere yew can see dem," she said. "Yew terrible man, yew. Yust go. I don't care vere."

"But my dear lady, it's after midnight," protested Amos Vachter. "Where am I to go this time of night?"

"Try da poorhouse, for all I care," said Hilma, and she turned back to the stairs and climbed them.

3

Backyard Bear

While Aunt Hilma was, by most accounts, a rather persnickety old lady, she continually fascinated David and me with her recollections of the harrowing adventures of lone woodsmen and farmers stalked in the dark of night by wolf packs near the family farm in Deerwood, Minnesota. She occasionally interchanged these stories with ones of Indians chasing those same woodsmen and farmers, but David and I didn't care. We seldom let the chance to hear a wolf story slip by even though frequently repeated.

Not by nature a storyteller, except on the subject of wolves and Indians—bears would be added to Hilma's repertoire later—most of the escapades she centered on her late uncles, August and Edmund, who survived encounters with wolves or Indians or both. In one especially satisfying experience, two Indians, who were angry with Uncle August, chased him, only to be detoured themselves and chased by a wolf.

August, who must have had a provoking manner, twice

21

was hounded by wolves, one time necessitating that he take cover in a neighbor's root cellar all night while the wolf pack clawed at the door and howled in its eagerness to devour him.

I think Hilma enjoyed the attention David and I gave her whenever she told her stories. But some of the luster left the wolf tales after bears began making early autumn forays into Duluth's residential neighborhoods during the late 1940s and early 1950s. The bruins, frustrated by poor berry crops, ambled into town, overturning garbage cans and wolfing down the edible contents. Police treed and shot several of them, while others were trapped for zoos or returned to the wilds outside of town.

Hilma minimized the threat posed by the intruders. "Dat's nutting," she noted authoritatively one morning. "Yew should of seen tings up to Deerwood ven ve vas kids. Den ve had da volfs. A bear is nutting. But a volf, now yew got someting."

She started in on another yarn, but my mother made her stop. "It's bad enough," Mother said, "that folks living in the heart of the city have to be concerned with bears, let alone scared half out of their wits by apocryphal stories of wolves."

I, of course, didn't know what "apocryphal" meant, and neither, I suspected, did Hilma. "Vell, bears is yust pups compared to volfs," Hilma sniffed. "I don't pay no mind to bears."

A day or so later Hilma was in the back yard hanging laundry on the line and gossiping to Olga Engqvist about the bear invasion.

Olga, who had during the several years following her husband Earl's death taken up the role as the neighborhood's chief eccentric by appearing in public in Earl's old clothes, was in her own back yard adjacent to Grandma's, wearing Earl's denim bib overalls and his straw skimmer. She chewed on a rhinestone-studded cigarette holder that had belonged to Earl, though she had never smoked. Taking the cigarette holder in her hand and gesturing with it for emphasis, she described the escapades of a bear running through our very yards. "Jackie Miller said he saw it run right across the alley," Olga said. "A big black one."

Hilma scoffed. She placed no stock in the stories, and said, "Vell, vit all my experience vit volfs, I'd yust tell a bear to shoo!"

Suddenly the color drained from Olga's face. "Hilma!" she whispered hoarsely. "There's a bear right now by your garbage can."

I heard Hilma's frightened yelp from our upstairs balcony where I was about to start beating rugs, and saw the bear casually nosing the trash can. He was scarcely more than a cub, but definitely a real bear—the first of the invaders I'd seen.

"Hilma—" I shouted. "Get out of there!"

The old woman was catatonic. "Mom!" I called, dashing downstairs. "There's a bear in Grandma's back yard and Hilma is out there!"

Mother raced to the window, then to our own back door. "Hilma!" she cried. "Oh, Hilma."

Hilma didn't move. The bear, some thirty feet away, moseyed about. He hadn't noticed Hilma, or, if he had, judged the contents of the can more appetizing than an elderly Swedish lady.

Weakly, Hilma reached back without taking her eyes off the bruin and picked a wooden clothespin from the sack hanging on the line. She held it out in front of her to ward off the bear, which still seemed ignorant of her presence. Slowly she crept toward Olga's garage, where one end of her clothesline was attached. She meant to sneak behind the garage through Fred Dingle's yard to the relative safety of Olga's yard, which was separated from hers by a white picket fence.

Mr. Dingle, fearing neighbor boys might use the natural pathway between the houses as a bike crossing and mow down his hollyhocks, had strung barbed wire between Olga's garage and his own shrubbery, inhibiting bike traffic, but also blocking Hilma's escape. She could not make it back to her house without arousing attention from the bear, which had, by then, tipped the garbage can.

Emboldened by the picket fence protection, Olga stepped forward. "Well now, Mr. Bear," she began. "You can just go back where you came from."

The bear's jaws clanked around an empty pork and beans can.

Olga, unaware of Fred Dingle's barbed wire fence, motioned for Hilma to circle behind her garage and get into her back yard.

By this time, Mother had phoned the police, telling them about the bear and that her aunt was in imminent danger.

"Just beat it," Mrs. Engqvist shouted emphatically, and tossed the cigarette holder at the bear. He gulped down two slices of moldly bread, snuffed about several more empty tins and jars, licking at this one and that. "Go through by the garage, for heaven's sake, Hilma," Olga called desperately. "I'm keeping him occupied here."

"Fence," Hilma croaked, with an odd gesture of her head.

At that moment the bear turned and noticed her. Hilma thrust the clothespin toward him as he lumbered forward.

Whatever thoughts the bear entertained were interrupted by a police siren, and as the car pulled into the driveway the bear dashed across our yard and into the alley. Hilma steadied herself against the clothes pole as one officer rushed to her, and the other gave chase after the bear.

Soon it seemed the entire neighborhood descended on Grandma's back yard, besieging Hilma with questions. Small boys got down on all fours and played bear with one another. Older men stood in the driveway, smoked cigarettes, and smiled enigmatically. Hilma, who had never received so much attention, definitely did not enjoy the spotlight. Pale and sweating, she asked for a drink of water.

Meanwhile, Mrs. Engqvist was calmly explaining how she had tried to divert the bear at some risk to herself, but that Hilma, poor thing, was unable to climb Fred Dingle's fence and make a getaway.

Finally Grandma and Mother helped Hilma back inside where she lay on the davenport and sipped Grandma's fresh lemonade.

Later, Uncle Howard stopped by. He relished opportunities to tease Hilma. For fun he would offer to let her dip into his snoose container, or present her with corncob pipes on her birthdays. Of course, under no circumstance would Hilma ever touch tobacco, and she would grow furious with him.

The bear episode amused Howard enormously. "Scared him off, hey, Hilma?" he asked. "Poor little fella. He was just looking for a friend. You know what they've been saying, don't you, Hilma? Them bears have been chased out of the woods by wolves. He probably heard about how you used to beat up on the wolves, and he wanted to snuggle up for a little protection." Howard chuckled and offered Hilma a chew.

"She scared him off with a clothespin," I said, capturing the spirit of the moment.

"Vat vould yew haf done?" Hilma said, glaring.

"If you chewed, you could have spit in his eye," Howard said.

"Yah, and den dat vould of been da end of me, I can tell yew."

"Is a bear as mean as a wolf?" I asked.

"That's not the question, Mickey," Howard said. "It isn't whether a bear is as mean as a wolf, but whether Hilma is as mean as a bear. She run him off, so I guess we know the answer to that, don't we?"

"It's not funny, Howard," Hilma said.

Her wolf stories grew less intense, less frequent from then on, with bears figuring more prominently.

"Yah, a volf, yew know right avay vat he's going to do," she said. "He vants to chew yew right down. But vit a bear, yew newer know for sure vat he's after. Yew don't vant to go messing vit no bears, I tell yew. Yust leaf me be from da volfs and da bears.

4

Learning to Spit for Distance

I customarily hopped next door to Grandma's each morning after breakfast to take a quick look at the sports section of the Duluth *News Tribune*, the city's morning newspaper. We subscribed to the evening *Herald*, but avid baseball fan that I was, I couldn't wait until late afternoon to peruse box scores from the previous day's games.

Fresh-baked cookies always accompanied my reading, as well as comments from Aunt Hilma on the goings on in the neighborhood, especially the latest happenings in the life of Olga Engqvist.

One morning as I pored over a profile of Stan Musial, Hilma snorted her disgust over Olga's behavior. "I tink she's gone nuts if yew ask me," she said. "Did you see her? She's all done up like a man again. She's on da porch right now lewking like a fool. I yust don't know vat's got into dat voman." Hilma shook her head.

I abandoned the paper and went to Grandma's front porch to peer across into the Engqvist yard. Hilma was right.

Mrs. Engqvist wore a pair of Earl's old gabardine slacks, inches too large at the waist, and tied with clothesline inserted through the belt loops. The bottoms were rolled two or three times at the ankles, revealing a pair of her late husband's old black brogans. Over her shoulders she wore her own orange winter coat, though it was July, and one of Earl's gray fedoras fastened to her head by a frayed maroon scarf wrapped over the hat and cinched beneath her chin. She noticed me and waved. "Well, hello there, Mickey," she called, smiling. She wore a vivid maroon lipstick, fashioned beyond her lip line, reaching scant millimeters below her nose.

Hilma stepped onto the porch, joining me. She shook her head again, while at the same time offering Mrs. Engqvist a polite wave. "Yew see? Yesterday she vent downtown lewking like dat. Plenty of folks yust stare at her dese days. I vunder if Yulie knows vat she's up tew?" Julie was Mrs. Engqvist's daughter, married and living in another state.

Until then I had simply regarded Mrs. Engqvist as the woman who lived next door to Grandma. She'd had her crotchets, but no more than many of the other elderly residents of the neighborhood.

"Vell, I newer seen nutting like it before, Mickey," Hilma told me several days later. "Olga Engqvist was playing marbles vit da Miller boy. Right down on da ground vit da boy. I tink somebody should call Yulie."

"There's nothing wrong with marbles," I said.

"Nutting wrong? Dey vas playing for keeps. She's teaching dat boy to gamble and she ought to know better dan dat."

"They're only having fun," I said. "Tell you what, Hilma. I'll teach you to play marbles too. Then you and Mrs. Engqvist can have your own tournament."

She snorted.

"I'll let you have my best shooter," I continued. "I'll go and tell Mrs. Engqvist that you think you can beat her at marbles."

"Yew will not," Hilma asserted crossly.

"She's wearing a lucky hat, Hilma. If we found a lucky hat for you, you could beat her. I'll bet Dad has an old one he'd let you have." I collapsed in a nine-year-old's silliness at the prospect of my old great aunt wearing one of my father's hats.

"I ain't playing vit no marbles," she huffed.

A week or so later, Mrs. Engqvist, wearing sailor cap and pea coat, came to call on Grandma and Hilma. It was a warm afternoon and the women sat on the porch. I had come on an errand for my mother, accompanied by my cousin, Deke, who was visiting.

Mrs. Engqvist hailed me. "Hello there, Mickey. And who's your young friend?"

"He's my cousin from Northfield," I said.

"Cousin, huh? Does he have a name?"

Deke, a quarrelsome, irksome boy a year younger than I, was precocious beyond his years. Tall, spindly, blond-haired, he was inept at rough-and-tumble games, and Mother made me promise to be nice to him. Unfortunately, no one exacted a similar promise from Deke. "My name is Whitney Brandt the Third," he announced haughtily. "But you may call me Deke."

"It is indeed nice to meet you, Deke," Mrs. Engqvist said. "Any friend of Mickey's is a friend of mine."

"Well, I'm not a friend of his. We're cousins—actually cousins thrice removed, through no fault of my own. And you couldn't say any cousin of his is a cousin of yours, could you?"

"Say, aren't you the clever one," said Mrs. Engqvist. She turned to Grandma. "Gustie, have you ever?"

Grandma merely nodded; Hilma had moved away and was staring out at the street.

"And how are you enjoying your visit, young man?" Mrs. Engqvist pressed pleasantly.

"It would be okay if there were more to do," Deke replied sourly, frowning.

"I know lots of things to do," said Mrs. Engqvist. "Just thousands and tons of things to do around here."

"I haven't seen any of them," Deke said, sullen.

"Well, Mickey likes to play ball. Some of the boys climb trees or just spit on the sidewalks to see who can spit the farthest."

"Ish," said Hilma.

"The only time you expectorate," Deke said, "is to get rid of something unpleasant in your mouth."

"You've never spit for fun?" Mrs. Engqvist asked. "Why, you don't know what you're missing. A fellow can't be a boy if he doesn't like to spit."

"Don't bodder da boys vit no spitting," Hilma said. "Yew get them tinking about chewing and spitting da snoose."

Mrs. Engqvist wrinkled her nose. "Oh, no, never. Why, gentlemen never chew tobacco. And these two are fine young gentlemen. This is just good clean fun, Hilma."

"Isn't clean," Hilma rasped, turning away again.

"Of course it is," Mrs. Engqvist said. "Now let's go outside. I'll be first."

"Yew're not going to mess on our sidevalk?" Hilma asked.

Mrs. Engqvist assured her we wouldn't, and just to make certain, we'd skip next door to her place.

She excused herself and held the door open for Deke and me, and we dashed across the front lawn to her front porch. "But first," she said, "I want to show you something."

She'd been landscaping the back yard and wondered what we thought of it. We followed her out back and saw the lawn partially torn up. The old lilac shrubs, which separated her yard from the Tenth Street sidewalk, had been dug up. They stood in root-ball clumps in her driveway. "What do you think?"

"It looks like the dew has dropped," Deke said.

"He thinks it looks like the dew has dropped," Mrs. Engqvist repeated, clapping her hands to her cheeks. "I don't know what I'm going to fill in where the lilacs were, but I just wanted to see what the yard looked like without them. Now the dew dropping . . . well, I never. I wouldn't have thought that, would you, Mickey?"

"I don't even know what that means," I said.

"It's an open metaphor," Deke said.

I didn't know what that meant either, nor, I suspected, did Mrs. Engqvist. Then she led us around to the front yard where we took seats on her porch steps.

"Now, Deke, you'll like this, you really will. First of all, you have to work up a base." She cleared her throat, leaned forward and sent forth a small glob, which landed some ten feet out on the sidewalk. "Now, you try it, Whitney."

Deke looked at her, then harrumphed and coughed; his face reddened. A great rushing noise parted his lips, but the spit smeared his chin, and he had to stand quickly, legs apart, lest it drip onto his trousers. His face still red, he wiped his chin and cursed.

"There'll be no more of that language, young man," Mrs. Engqvist scolded. "I'll forgive it this once as a mistake, but no more." She touched my arm. "Now you try, Mickey."

I pursed my lips and shot a stream forward about five or six feet, where it bubbled on the walk.

"Not bad," she said. "But I still lead."

Deke tried again, clearing his chin this time, but not managing to propel the spittle beyond the bottom step of the porch.

Mrs. Engqvist sighed. "Don't use your tongue, Deke. Just gather a bit of air in your cheeks to push it." She demonstrated and another blob landed in the vicinity of the first. "Not bad for an old woman," she said. "I guess I'm the champion. Hip-hip—hooray," she shouted, and laughed.

She retreated to the house and returned with several glasses and a pitcher of water, for moisture retention, she said. We sipped and spat, sipped and spat, until, finally, I squirted a mouthful at Deke, who promptly returned the favor. Within seconds we were soaking each other. Mrs. Engquist joined in, her laughter rolling in great peals down the block.

Hilma, of course, was appalled as we went back to Grandma's house to complete the errand that Mother had sent us on perhaps an hour earlier.

After supper that evening, Hilma came to our house. "I don't know vat yew folks tink, but I tink Olga is crazy. Yew should of seen how she had Mickey and Deke spitting all ower da sidevalk. Dey spit on each udder tew. And so did she. Da voman's nuts, if yew ask me."

"She's harmless," my father said.

Hilma disagreed. "She's got da boys playing keeps vit marbles, and she's teaching 'em to spit. Next ting yew know, Mickey vill be gambling and chewing snoose."

I had been playing keeps with marbles for at least three years already. And when I chewed tobacco—six or seven years later—it was a one-time experience. I swallowed the chew and felt nauseated all day.

5

The Saturday Cowboys

When I knew him, Hjalmer Severson was a thirtyish man-child; man in size and age, but child in mind. Along with hundreds of other kids, he regularly attended the Saturday morning serials during the late 1940s that were featured at the Lyric and Lyceum theaters in Duluth. And like multitudes of young fans of Gene Autry, Hoot Gibson, or Eddie Dean, Hjalmer came to each show attired in cowboy garb, replete with two imitation pearl-handled cap pistols and lariat.

During action scenes, he and other kids whipped out their firearms, took cover behind seats or pillars and blazed away at the screen. They never remained fixed, but dashed about the theater, hollering encouragement to Roy, Gene and their own peers, vaulting over seats, racing to the nether reaches of the balcony in order to gain better vantage, while making onamatapoetic sounds of gunfire—"Pow—pow—pow!"

Not everyone in the theater tolerated the continual cacophony well. Some of us hoped to hear the dialogue, which the gunfighters rendered inaudible.

It was difficult for other youthful patrons not to react whenever some varmint sneaked up on Gabby Hayes, who had been ordered to post watch. Suddenly, half the audience leaped to their feet, screaming, "Look out—look out! He's right behind you, Gabby!"

The other half bellowed, "Shut up! Sit down and shut up!" And for several minutes the screen dialogue invariably submerged under the hysterical cries of "Look out!" and "Shut up!"

During the course of the picture, Hjalmer criss-crossed the entire theater, taking cover behind seats in each section, dashing down front to fire point-blank at rustlers or robbers, then retreating to the safety of the balcony. But where other kids roamed in small gangs, Hjalmer played alone. At the end of each Saturday segment, Hjalmer exited the theater pale and sweating.

He wore the same uniform each week with one variation; in the winter he donned fleece chaps, which were too warm for summer. Otherwise he had his aqua cowboy shirt with white trim and white bandana. He wore blue jeans, tan boots, and his white Stetson.

The others who played in the theater regarded Hjalmer with suspicion. He was clearly an adult, but did not behave like one. Now and again a youngster might step behind a pillar to reload and find Hjalmer there with similar intent. The kid would stare for an embarrassed moment, then leave, pondering for several seconds what he just encountered before resuming his play.

When the lights were turned on about 11:00 a.m., most of us cheered and left the theater in high spirits, joking, talking about the films, or trying out leaps we had seen and mock punches like those thrown by Hoot or Hoppy.

Hjalmer was always hyper, agitated. An usher spied him in the drinking fountain line after one morning's show. He grinned and said, "How's the war, Hjalmer?"

"Real tough," Hjalmer said, nodding.

"But you can take it, hey, Hjalmer?"

"Yeah, I can take it," Hjalmer said, patting his revolvers.

The usher laughed and nudged one of his fellow ushers. Hjalmer smiled.

One Saturday during a chase scene involving Roy Rogers and Andy Devine, Hjalmer was "shot" from behind and pitched forward near my aisle seat. "Winged me," Hjalmer rasped and untied his bandana. He cinched it around his left bicep. "I'm all right," he called out. "I'm okay." He scrambled to his feet, turned and fired more shots at the screen.

"Did you see that?" brother David asked. "That man is as big as Dad." David was incredulous and wanted to talk about it at home. He had to be careful, however, not to discuss Hjalmer or any aspect of movies in front of Hilma, who maintained that people who made moving pictures and people who attended them were doomed to an eternity with Satan in Hell.

David was too young to think about that, but he seemed less interested in the serials after witnessing the "shooting of Hjalmer," and a great deal more interested in watching the antics of this very odd man.

One spring Saturday morning at the Lyceum, about midway through the show, David nudged me. "Look at him. He's down there in front, and some bigger boys are tying him up."

Several teenage boys had taken Hjalmer's lariat and tied him hands and feet, then rolled him down the aisle to the front of the stage. A number of kids laughed when they saw Hjalmer.

From then on, whenever certain boys were bored with the picture, they'd group together, find Hjalmer and tie him up. This practice continued throughout the summer.

Even the teenage ushers seemed to enjoy the ritual capture and binding of Hjalmer. It was, however, never a game to Hjalmer, who writhed on the floor for up to ten minutes sometimes, before somebody freed him.

Once I was near an usher who untied Hjalmer in the balcony. "Them guys ain't fair," Hjalmer whimpered. "I shot 'em, but they wouldn't fall down."

"Crooks don't play fair, Hjalmer," the usher said. "You ought to be able to take care of yourself. You're bigger than they are."

"But them are mean," Hjalmer said.

Several weeks later, David and I returned to the Lyceum and waited in a lengthy line for another adventure flick. Several positions ahead of us stood Hjalmer Severson. A slight rain fell, and he kept looking up at it, his eyes blinking madly as droplets hit them.

As usual, kids jostled one another in line, shouted, and wrestled. David and I noticed Hjalmer turn around, anguish mapped on his vapid face, his arms raised above his head in the manner of one being held up.

"Keep 'em up, Hjalmie-palmie," a boy in a tattered baseball cap said. He was behind Hjalmer, his finger jammed into Hjalmer's lower back.

"What'll we do with him, Artie?" another boy called.

"Let's string him up," shouted a third kid.

"Tell you what," the one named Artie said, smirking, "we'll hogtie him." He reached for Hjalmer's lariat and removed it from his belt. "Now—"

"No, not the rope," Hjalmer pleaded. "Don't tie me up." He dropped his arms. "Here, take my money. A dollar." He thrust it toward Artie, who snatched it and, with his friends, dashed toward the rear of the line.

"Now we don't have to pay nothin', Artie," one of them yelled. They laughed as they ran past David and me.

David and I did nothing, said nothing. We watched Hjalmer cross the street and disappear into the Greyhound Bus Depot.

6

Bert Carlson's Winch

Bert Carlson, who lived across the street from us, and Uncle Howard were both chronically unemployed. Because of that they endured frequent neighborhood opprobrium. Naturally, therefore, they formed a bond of sorts and enjoyed one another's company. Often when Howard supposedly stopped by to visit Grandma, he'd spend only a few obligatory moments there before heading over to Bert's house. Then the two of them would while away a summer's afternoon sitting on Bert's front steps in their undershirts, smoking hand-rolled Bull Durham cigarettes and drinking beer from cans.

In appearance they formed an unlikely pair. Howard was rail thin, but sinewy, with a full, luxuriant head of russet hair; Bert was fat in a peculiar sort of way. His arms and legs were rather spindly, but his belly was immense. And he was bald, except for a sparse blond fringe.

"Yust lewk at da tew of dem," Hilma remarked one sultry afternoon, shuddering with disgust. "Needer vun of dem vit a yob, sitting dere and yacking avay about nutting. Ish."

Grandma, seated on the porch swing next to Hilma, said nothing, as was her custom whenever Hima verbally scourged Howard, Grandma's only surviving son.

"Yew'd tink he'd know better, Gustie," Hilma continued. "He's had ewery adwantage, and lewk at him. Vasting his time vit dat no gewd Bert."

Grandma, who spoke ill of no one at any time, said, "It seems to me Bert has lost some weight lately."

"Uff. Hasn't needer. Fat as a valrus. Fatter, maybe." Hilma shook her head. "I hate to say it, Gustie, but dey're bums, da bote of dem."

Even so, some of their exploits used to amuse me, even if these same exploits enraged Hilma and my mother.

Bert was a gadgeteer of the first order. When he did leave his front steps, it was usually to fondle and expound the virtues of some gadget he'd recently purchased. No matter what the newfangled object was, it always irked Mom. "How can he afford something like that, Mike?" she asked Dad, spying Bert in his front yard with a new power mower. "How in the world can he buy that?"

"He probably charged it," Dad said.

"Hah. I know his type. He'll use it all summer and have it repossessed come fall because he hasn't made any payments."

After lunch one day, I was summoned to Grandma's to help Hilma board the bus and escort her downtown to the Medical Arts Building. She had recently fallen on the steps and required a doctor's appointment.

Howard, seated at the kitchen table when I arrived, apparently just had offered to drive Hilma downtown himself. Before Hilma could answer, a loud knock came on the front door.

That morning, Bert had made a particularly pleasing purchase at Montgomery Ward's and was anxious to try it out.

Upon noticing Howard's 1939 Chevy in the driveway, he'd lumbered over to engage his pal. "Howie, I'd sort of like to have you see something," Bert said, an awkward grin filling his florid face.

"Like to, Bert," Howard said, but I've just promised Auntie here I'd take her downtown for her doctor's appointment."

"No problem. I'll drop her off myself. Got a couple errands to run, and then I can show you this certain thingamajig."

"Well, if it's okay with Hilma, it's fine with me," said Howard.

"No bodder," Hilma said. "I can yust as easy take da bus."

"Wouldn't think of it, Auntie," Bert said. "We'll drive you first class." He glanced down at me. "Shoot, the kid can come along too, if he'd like."

I needed no further encouragement. I much preferred a ride in Bert's DeSoto to one on a dusty city bus. Hilma thought maybe I should stay home, or at least tell my mother. I said it wouldn't be necessary, knowing how Mom felt about Bert and even Howard, and especially the two of them together.

Now Bert was a fast driver. He had never outgrown his teenage hotrodding, and routinely jerked to stop signs, laying a little rubber as he pulled away. Nobody said anything, but Hilma, sitting with me in the back seat, whitened perceptibly and continually pulled on her hankie with both hands.

"Yew can yust let us out ven ve get to Superior Street," Hilma whispered.

"Oh, no, Auntie," said Bert. "Wouldn't think of it. We'll bring you right to the door and get you on the elevator."

"I vouldn't bodder if I vas yew," Hilma said.

"You're going to be early, Hilma," Howard said. "You got plenty of time. Don't worry about a thing."

Bert asked when Hilma's appointment was, and Howard said quarter past two. It was only one-thirty.

"Lotsa time, lotsa time," Bert said. "Listen, Howie, we

got enough time to let me show you this little item I was mentioning. You don't mind, Auntie?" he called back over his shoulder. "You got plenty of time."

"I don't vant tew be late," Hilma said weakly, as Bert maneuvered around a semi. The truck driver pulled his air horn in appreciation of Bert's skills. Bert chuckled. Hilma gasped.

Bert drove us down across the Aerial Lift Bridge onto Park Point. He sped at forty-five miles an hour toward the end of the point, and pulled the car off the road onto a stretch of sand beach, where he began racing.

"What in the world are you doing?" Howard cried. "We got the old lady and Mickey here, for crying out loud."

Poor Hilma paled; spittle had gathered at the corner of her mouth. Her hands folded in supplication, and her eyes closed tightly. My heart thundered in my throat, and I sat very near my great aunt.

"In a minute, in a minute," Bert called, whereupon the heavy car sank in soft sand up to the frame. Bert revved the engine and tried to spin out, but the car didn't move.

"Now you've done it, Bert," Howard said irritably. "We have to get her to the doc's, and you got us stuck instead. How'll we ever get out of here?"

Bert grinned. "That's what I was gonna show you, Howard. Got a neat little ticketybob in the trunk that'll pull us out of here in a jiff." Still beaming, he bounded out of the car and opened the trunk. He withdrew a winch. "Got this baby at Monkey Wards," he said. "Watch how this little honey works, Howard."

Howard helped Hilma from the car. I had scrambled out as soon as Bert had opened the trunk. Hilma, dressed in her black linen dress and coat, drew as many stares from gawking picnickers as did the shiny DeSoto sunk in the sand.

"You'll have to hurry, Bert," Howard said, and gave an apologetic little shrug to Hilma, who pursed her lips.

"Nothing to it," Bert said, and he fastened one end of the

winch to the bumper and anchored it to a nearby tree. "Now watch this. These things are really neat. Everybody ought to have one. No kidding." He cranked the handle and tightened the wire. The car quivered momentarily. Bert cranked again. The car didn't move. He continued cranking on the winch, finally producing a great creaking. "Now we got her coming," he called. He was red-faced, perspiring profusely. Again he cranked, both hands on the grip. We heard a heavy groan and creak. "Ah-h-h," Bert said, pleased.

Suddenly the tree anchoring the winch was pulled out by the roots and crashed onto the roof of Bert's car. Bert cursed mightily, and Howard began laughing. The car never budged.

"You think it's funny, Howard?" Bert cried. "I ought to bust you on the snotlocker."

"You'd have to catch me first," Howard said, chuckling.

Hilma and I wandered over to the gaping hole from which the tree had sprung. "Yiminy," Hilma said. "Yew could stuff a long dawenport down dere and have room left ower."

"My car is ruined," Bert moaned, and he sat on the beach, head in hands.

Howard stopped laughing. "We'll just have to call a wrecker, Bert," he said.

"Yeah, and who's going to pay for it? I don't have no money."

"Your insurance will take care of it. Don't worry."

"I don't have no insurance, Howard," Bert said. He seemed on the verge of tears. "All I got is that damn winch."

Meanwhile, two o'clock arrived. Hilma fumed because she would miss her appointment, and had worn her good dress and had sand in her shoes. "Yust my luck to get stuck vit dose fools," she huffed.

"It's all right," I said. "We can take a bus from here right downtown."

She brightened briefly and made a dignified attempt to walk through the sand up to Minnesota Avenue. "I newer seen nutting like it, Mickey. Nobody but yewr uncle and dat fatty vould ewer do someting so dumb."

We were only five minutes late for her appointment. Howard and Bert wrestled with the car for the rest of the afternoon, until an area resident pulled them out with his truck. They arrived home about 8:30, soiled and sullen. Howard came directly to Grandma's to wash up before heading to his own apartment.

"Vell, dat didn't take so long, I see," Hilma said, smirking.

Howard glared at her an instant, but said nothing. He emptied a fistful of Bab-O cleanser into his hand and began scrubbing himself in the kitchen sink.

7

"Tousands and Millions of Rats"

The day the rats came up through the storm sewers on Tenth Avenue East and Tenth Street, another Swedish neighbor, Dagney Ahlstrom rushed across the street to Grandma's and burst in screaming, 'Ve got rats! Tousands and millions of rats!"

Hilma, aghast that Mrs. Ahlstrom had barged in without knocking, rolled down her sweater sleeves and looked away as she fussed with her hair to make herself presentable. "Rats?" she said, turning to Mrs. Ahlstrom.

"Rats?" I echoed, looking up from the Monday morning box scores. "There aren't any rats around here."

"Oh, yew're wrong, Mickey," Mrs. Ahlstrom said. "Yew're qvite terribly wrong. Ve got rats all right. Ve got 'em right here. I newer seen da like, Hilma."

"Rats?" Hilma asked again, and sat at the table. "Gustie," she called to Grandma. "Yew better hear dis. Dagney says ve got rats."

Mrs. Ahlstrom loosened the scarf around her face. She

was perhaps seventy, her face wrinkled with deep crevices among the folds of fat. "Mrs. Danielson called dis morning and told me to be careful as can be ven I go outside because dere's rats on da street."

"Gustie," Hilma called again, urgently. "First ve got bears and now rats. Vat in da vorld is wrong, anyway?"

"Isn't da half of it, Hilma," Mrs. Ahlstrom said. "Yew know ven rats start coming into da neighborhood, it means dere isn't anyting for dem to eat in da dumps and sewers anymore. It means dey'll be in our homes eating our food, and—" Her voice broke, and she sat down, entwining her blue satin scarf in her fingers. "Dey could ewen eat *us*, Hilma. Mickey here might be able to run avay, but us older vuns, ve'd be no match for dem. And den, yew got da end of da vorld is vat yew got."

Grandma entered the kitchen from the basement where she'd been washing clothes. Hilma tossed her a look of agitation for taking so long. "Well, Dagney," Grandma said, and smiled.

"Rats," Hilma said.

"Rats?"

"Yes, Gustie," said Mrs. Ahlstrom. "Dere's rats all ower Tent Street, and I vouldn't be tew qvick tew run down into dat basement anymore needer. It may be full of dem."

"My word, what are you talking about?" Grandma asked.

"Rats," said Mrs. Ahlstrom. "Da neighborhood, maybe ewen da whole city is inwaded by rats. Here, come lewk."

She led us outside and took several steps up Tenth Avenue. Other neighbors gathered a few feet from the intersection on Tenth Street, pointing and gesturing.

Olga Engqvist stood on her front porch idly twirling one of her late husband's straw skimmers on her index finger. She waved at us. "Come see the rats," she called pleasantly.

It was true; dozens of small brown rats scurried to and fro in and out of the storm sewer grates on either side of Tenth Street. Bert Carlson smoked a cigarette while, with detached amusement, he watched the carryings on of the rodents.

"What you been feeding them, Olga," he called. "You got a fine healthy crop up there."

"Cheese and bits of bacon," Olga shouted back. "That brings them around every time. You know, Bert, we could have a real show if you'd get your flute and start playing. You could be the Pied Piper of Duluth." She laughed.

"How can dey yoke at a time like dis?" Hilma said.

I continued up the hill to get a closer look. Other kids caterwauled in the street, tossing pebbles at the rats, which were picking up seeds helicoptering down from overhead maples.

"Rats don't eat seeds," Bert remarked to no one in particular. He had ambled up the hill behind me, standing about a dozen feet back of the intersection, his breathing labored, his great belly heaving. Though perpetually jobless, he seldom tended his five young sons, who were minded by a sitter who arrived at his house around seven most mornings, when Carleen, Bert's wife, went off to work.

Bert normally rose about noon and sagged into his front steps, where he'd crack a can of beer and watch the world according to Tenth Avenue pass by. Which was to say a few cars and kids on bikes. He'd sit in his undershirt, trousers, and slippers, drink a few beers and smoke cigarettes.

But now one of his small sons crept up behind him as Bert watched the rats. He turned on the little fellow. "Get in the house," he barked, and grunted as he leaned down to pick up a stone. He heaved it in the general direction of a cluster of rats, plinking one of them. The rodents scattered as Bert yelped gleefully. "Jeez, ya see that? I nailed the little bugger." He turned around facing the neighbors. "Nipped him. Ya see that?" He bent for another rock and threw it, but it landed nowhere near the other feeding rats.

Finally a municipal truck arrived and connected hoses to the fire hydrant.

"They're going to give them rats a bath," Bert called.

"We're gonna have the cleanest rats in Duluth right here."

Gallons of water were forced into the sewers for the rest of the morning, and no one saw any rats. But fifteen minutes after the truck departed, the rats were back, up like jacks-in-the box, sleek and shiny.

"Fat Bert vas right," moaned Mrs. Ahlstrom. "Dey give da rats a nice bat, dat's all dey did. And I seen some of dem go in Olga's yard. Yew don't suppose she's feeding dem do yew? It'd be yust like her. She's nutty enough tew dew it. And dat cat of her's is scared of dem. Von't make a move. Yew'd tink a cat vould be in his glory. But not dat stinker she got."

"Vy can't dey yust poison dem?" Hilma asked.

"We could get some cheese and put out traps," I ventured.

"Uff—yew'd be lucky to catch tree or four of dem," Mrs. Ahlstrom said. "I called da police. Maybe dey'll shoot dem."

"Maybe Hilma could throw a clothespin at them," I said, giggling.

"Dat vouldn't dew no gewd, Mickey," Mrs. Ahlstrom said. "Vat a silly idea."

"Well, she scared a bear with one once."

"Newer mind about da bears," said Hilma. "Rats can bite yew and give yew diseases. Ve don't need yewr teasing needer."

A police car pulled up, and a scowling, overweight officer got out.

"Just a few rats, officer," said Bert with studied nonchalance.

"A few rats, my foot," huffed Hilma.

"More like a million of dem," Mrs. Ahlstrom said. "I'm frightened dey might get into my house."

"Try to think of the rats as bunnies," Olga said, marching down from her porch to join us. "My encyclopedia says that rabbits are rodents. Rats are rodents. They're related, don't you see. You wouldn't be upset with rabbits, so don't get worked up about rats either. They're actually very fascinating to watch. I bet you could get them to feed right out of your hand, given time."

"Ve don't need dat kind of time, Olga," Hilma snapped.

Mrs. Ahlstrom drew circles around her ear with her forefinger for the officer's benefit and indicated Mrs. Engqvist. "Vill yew shoot dem, officer?" she asked.

"We aren't gonna shoot anything, lady," he said. "The health department says these things happen every once in a while, and that it's nothing to get excited about. Just keep your doors tightly closed. These rats are in storm sewers, not your sewer pipes. They won't come up through your toilets or manholes. Now the city is going to drop poison bait into the sewers, and they think that'll take care of the problem in a day or so. In the meantime, just stay calm and keep away from the rats."

"Yah, dat's easy for yew to say," said Mrs. Ahlstrom. "Yew don't live here."

"I'm sorry, lady," he said. "That's all I can do."

He got into his car and drove slowly up to the intersection, which Bert suggested ought to be renamed Rat Run Drive. I was the only one who laughed at the idea, and quickly passed it on to my friends.

In the meantime, the rodents loitered in the intersection for several more days, making themselves unwelcome and drawing gawkers from other unplagued neighborhoods.

Hilma took to jamming towels around door frames in the house, and whenever she ventured into the bathroom, she carried a heavy toilet plunger. "Da folks down in city hall, dey say if yew find a rat in yewr toilet yew should sock him vit da plunger and hold him under vater till he drowns. I hope I can do dat before I faint dead avay."

Five days later, it occured to everyone that nobody had seen a rat in a day or two. The invasion apparently had ended; the rats retreated back to the waterfront, or perhaps the poison had worked.

Aunt Ada had called Howard and told him about the excitement with the rats, but by the time he stopped by, the hoopla already had died. "Gee, I'm sorry to have missed out on all the fun," he said.

"Didn't miss nutting," Hilma said.

"Well, golly," Howard said, tapping tobacco into his corncob pipe. "I feel cheated. It's not every day something like this happens in the old neighborhood."

"Vell, dey're all gone now," said Hilma.

"I don't want to sound like an alarmist, Hilma, but that don't necessarily mean your troubles are over."

Hilma looked up. "Vat do yew mean?"

Slowly, deliberately, Howard struck fire to his pipe and sucked on it, sending clouds of Union Leader smoke toward the living room chandelier. "I mean," Howard continued, "I've read where rats make a beeline out of a place whenever disaster is about to strike. Whenever you see rats beat it, you know something terrible is on the way. They can sense it. They got what you call intuition. So if I was you, I wouldn't be too happy to see those rats leave. It might mean something worse is on the way."

"Ooooh," Hilma groaned. "I tot if a body had her fill of volfs and bears and rats, da vorst vould be over. But I got vun dat beats all—a nephew dat teases."

8

Uncle Philemon's Proposal

One August morning in 1950, Olga Engqvist's Uncle Philemon came from Deerwood to visit. He had farmed all his working life and had known all the Norquists while they lived in Deerwood some years earlier. He had been rather well acquainted with Hilma's Uncle August, who had farmed in Deerwood until his death.

Because he had known August well, Philemon was most eager, said Mrs. Engqvist, to see Hilma again after nearly fifty years. She asked Grandma if they might stop over for a visit. From my usual place at the kitchen table before a plate of cookies and the *News Tribune* sports pages, I said I'd be very much interested in meeting an old codger with a name like Philemon.

"Don't be tew sure of dat, Mickey," Hilma said sourly. "Da man's a scoundrel. Ooooh, how he vas a bodder to Uncle August. He yust drove him nuts. And I'm not so happy to see him myself." She looked at Grandma, who was wiping dishes at the kitchen sink. "I tink I'll go upstairs ven dey come. I don't need to see dem."

"Oh, Hilma, he's awfully old now," said Grandma. "You can just let bygones be bygones. See him. Think how hurt Olga would be if you didn't."

Hilma stayed put and so did I. Several minutes later the door bell rang, and I answered it. Olga stood there with a wizened, white-haired man who held a black cane and wore a large hearing aid in his left ear. Olga greeted me and, in a loud voice, said, "Uncle Philemon, this young man is Mickey Fedo. He's Ramona's boy."

"Huh?" said Uncle Philemon, cupping his hand to his ear, and then extending it to me for shaking.

Olga did not repeat herself, but continued past me into the house, tugging the hand of her ancient uncle. "Good day, folks," she said, ushering Philemon into the kitchen. "I don't think you've ever met Gustie, Uncle, but I bet you remember Hilma."

The old man broke into a broad, toothless grin. "Hilma, Hilma," he said, and shook his head. "Why you're all grown up and old yourself."

"Uncle . . ." scolded Olga.

"Well, last time I seen her she was just becoming a young lady. Now look at her. She was the youngest of August's nieces, isn't that right? I got a good memory, and I remember all right. Whooee, I'd like to sit down," he said, and sat on one of the white wooden kitchen chairs.

"I'm glad to meet you," Grandma said.

"It's nice to see you again, Philemon," said Hilma flatly.

"He's a little tired from the bus ride," Olga said. "Do you know, he's eighty-six. Imagine that. Almost a hundred."

"I'm young yet," the old man said, nodding, smiling. He reached out with his cane and tapped Hilma's thigh. She frowned and slid her chair back beyond his reach.

Grandma brought in coffee and helped Philemon move closer to the table. He dunked cookies in his coffee and slurped them. He caught me watching him and winked. "When you ain't got teeth, you gotta drink the cookies with the coffee. What did you say your name was?"

"Mike," I said.

"That's Mickey," Mrs. Engqvist shouted. "Ramona's boy—I told you."

"Ramona?"

"Gustie's daughter. Hilma's niece. She's married to Mickey's daddy, big Mike Fedo. He's with the symphony orchestra. Splendid musician. You just can't beat him. Those Eye-talians have music in their blood. I've often said that, haven't I Gustie?"

Uncle Philemon's attention waned, and he returned to his cookies and the slurping. After he downed two or three of them, he wiped his mouth on his sleeve and sat back. "Hilma," he said, nodding in her direction. "I remember your Uncle August, Hilma. Queer fellow. Queer."

"Uncle, that's not nice," Olga said.

"I'm going to tell a little story about August now. The boy here would like to hear it. He never saw old August. August died long before you was born. How old are you, sonny?"

"Eleven."

"See, eleven. August been dead now must be thirty-five ... forty years. Queer fellow." He chuckled to himself, and the chuckle deepened until it became a rollicking laugh, which ended only when the old man began to cough—a heavy, catarrhous cough that reddened his face and brought tears to his rheumy eyes.

Grandma brought him a glass of water, and Olga patted him on the back. "You gave us a fright there, Uncle. You shouldn't get so excited."

He waved them off, swallowed the water and cleared his throat. "Hilma," he said. "Hilma. You remember August never went near to a bath tub. Never took no bath. Whooee, he was strong." Philemon pinched his nostrils with his right hand.

Hilma grunted and turned away, irritated. Olga nudged

her uncle. "That isn't pleasant, Uncle. Let's talk about something else."

The old fellow waved her off again. "Hilma, there was a couple Halloweens there when kids used to come over from all around and try tipping old August over. They'd try to move my biffy out there, but when they get to August's place, they leave the biffy and try to tip him. Hee-hee-hee," he laughed, a piercing, high-pitched giggle.

The women looked away, embarrassed, but I joined Philemon's laughter. "Maybe that's why wolves always chased Uncle August," I ventured. "He smelled like their food." That made Philemon laugh harder.

"Yew see vat I mean, Gustie?" Hilma whispered crossly to Grandma. "Yew see vy I newer cared to see him. Ask dem to leaf."

"But, Hilma," pressed Philemon. "I always liked August. He was a good friend and a good farmer to boot. Tell me, Hilma, do you ever think about going back to Deerwood?"

Hilma sighed. "Oh, I suppose I tink about it now and den, yah. But I been here now near to forty-five years. And da old place isn't da same needer."

"Deerwood's still the best," Philemon said. "You hear folks talk about God's country. Deerwood is God's country, far as I'm concerned." He tapped Hilma's thigh again with his cane. "You belong there, Hilma. You come back with me."

"Vat? Dat's crasy. Dis is vere I live now."

"I got a nice place right in town now, Hilma. You marry me, and we'll live right there in town."

A stunned silence engulfed the kitchen. The ticking of the grandfather clock in the living room was the only sound for several long seconds. Hilma crimsoned.

"Goodness," Grandma said finally.

"Now I believe I've heard everything," said Olga. "Uncle, what in the world has gotten into you?"

"Huh? I made Hilma a proposal of marriage." He nodded

forcefully and sat forward, both hands cupping the handle of his cane as it bore his weight against the floor.

Hilma remained speechless, color draining from her face. She reached for the water that had been placed before Philemon several minutes earlier and drank the rest of it. "I don't feel so gewd," she croaked. She stood and walked a bit unsteadily from the kitchen, climbed the stairs, went into her bedroom and closed the door.

"Uncle, you've upset poor Hilma," Olga said.

"Is that so?" He grinned. "I don't beat the bush," he said, grabbing another cookie.

But Olga stood. "Well," she said, "you've certainly embarrassed me this morning, Uncle. I never would have imagined."

Philemon beamed proudly, sucked down the last of the cookie, nodded at Grandma, and allowed Olga to take his arm and help him from his chair.

"Gustie, I just don't know what to say. I'm at a loss for words." Olga turned to me. "Mickey, have you ever?"

I shrugged, and they started for the door. As Olga pushed it open, Philemon said, "That August, he was a queer bird." Then they were gone.

Grandma sat down and fanned herself with a folded section of the morning newspaper. "Isn't that something?" she said. "Just imagine that." She smiled shyly. "Maybe you should have your mother come over here right away, Mickey," she said.

I ran home and hailed Mom. "That old uncle of Mrs. Engqvist's wants to marry Hilma and have her move back to Deerwood with him. Grandma wants you over there right away."

"Whaa—at? You're kidding," Mom said, wiping her hands on her apron and following me back to Grandma's.

Grandma related the incident as best she could and asked Mother what she thought. Mom said she didn't know; she was totally shocked and wondered if Hilma was all right.

She went upstairs and knocked on Hilma's door. "Hilma
. . . Hilma, are you okay?"

"Yust leaf me be a vile," Hilma called back. "Yust leaf
me be."

The phone rang downstairs, and Mother dashed down to
get it. It was Olga calling to apologize again. "I don't know
what's gotten into Uncle," she told Mother. "He certainly
is acting strange."

"Well, he's an old man," Mother said. "He'll probably
forget all about it by tomorrow."

Olga said she surely hoped so and wanted Mother to tell
Grandma and Hilma that she'd never in her life been so embarrassed.

Later that afternoon when Howard stopped by, he was
appraised of Hilma's offer. By then she had come out of her
room and was peeling potatoes in the kitchen. "I think you
should accept the old gentleman's offer, Hilma," Howard
said. "You're not getting any younger, you know."

"Yah, and needer is he," she snorted. "He's got vun foot
in da grave right now, if yew ask me."

Howard winked. "That's because he's cold, Hilma. You
could warm up those old bones of his."

"Oh, hush, Howard," she said, reddening.

"Well, it sounds like fun, Hilma. Mickey could get the
boys around here to give you a real shivaree."

Hilma huffed out of the kitchen.

Two days later, old Philemon came calling alone, struggling up the front steps to Grandma's porch. "Sonny?" he
said, peering at me as I left the house. "Have you met me?
You're sonny, ain't you? Whatsername's boy?"

"Yes," I said.

He smiled. "Well, how's my sweetheart today?"

"What?"

"Hilma. How's Hilma?"

"Fine, I guess."

"Can you help me with the door?" he asked. "I got rheumatism so bad sometimes I can't turn the handle on a door." He took my arm and leaned heavily against me as I guided him into the house.

"Ah, Hilma," he said, beaming.

Hilma fairly jumped from her living room rocker.

"Now, Hilma, I'll be going back to Deerwood tomorrow, and I'd be just as proud as a peacock if you'd come with me. There's all sorts of folks remember you there. We would have a lovely time together, Hilma. It's God's country, and you belong there."

Hilma didn't look at him for a long moment, and still didn't when she finally spoke. "Tank yew, no, Philemon. It vouldn't vork."

"I don't see why not."

Hilma flushed. "Because I don't love yew, Philemon. Now yust leaf me be."

"You're absolutely sure, are you, Hilma?"

"Yah. Yah, dere's no doubt."

"Ah," he said ruefully, then brightened as Grandma entered the room. "And you, lady, what about you? I forget your name."

"Well, I'm fine thank you, Philemon. Just fine."

"Yes, I can see that very well. My friend Hilma here has turned me down. So I'm free to inquire of you then, lady. Would you come to Deerwood with me?"

"Tell him no, Gustie," Hilma whispered. "Da old fool is nuts."

"Thank you, no," said Grandma.

"Well, why not? Why not, in heaven's name? I could provide for you—both you and Hilma. Why not? I'm getting discouraged." He looked at me. "The ladies will turn you inside out, sonny."

Grandma drew herself up and exhaled. "Well, I've been married once, and of course Eric's been dead a good long time. But I'm old now, too, and once was enough for me."

"I had two wives," Philemon said. "Outlived both of them. But I'm ready to try again. Only now nobody wants me. I don't understand it."

Olga burst through the front door. "Are you at it again, Uncle?"

"Now he wants to marry Grandma," I said.

"Take him over to Dagney's house, Olga," Hilma said.

"There's more?" the old man asked, brightening again. "Sure, let me see her. I tell you, Olga, I want a wife. If these ladies can't oblige me, show me one who will."

The two of them left then, and later, after he'd gone, Mrs. Engqvist said she'd never in her life spent such a week. "I used to think he was such a gentle old soul. But, my, he's got a lot of snap for an old fellow. He's going to correspond with Dagney. She said she'd write him. He's just as silly as a schoolboy. I hope the excitement won't be too much for him."

It may have been. Neighbors in Deerwood said he was up burning the midnight oil, attempting to craft letters to woo the winsome Dagney. Philemon came down with pneumonia in November and passed away shortly before Christmas.

9

Demolition Northern Pike

Throughout his adult life, Mother's brother Howard was an inveterate angler who spent many hours on lakes around Duluth, where he apparently took many large northern pike and walleyes. Occasionally he used to needle my father, who enjoyed only mediocre success. Howard's bragging rankled him, and he sometimes asked Howard for proof. Once in a while Howard produced a photo, but mostly he responded that the fish had been cleaned and given away to neighbors.

Dad strongly suspected Howard had fallen prey to the primal urge of most fishermen—lying. "There's no way he's catching fish that big in Fish Lake," Dad said. "That guy fishes with his mouth."

Howard knew what Dad thought of his fishing exploits, because Dad often told him to his face. Howard usually responded, "I'm not asking you to believe me, just come with me sometime. You'll see."

"Can't, Howard. I gotta work, you know." This barbed reference to Howard's perpetual joblessness usually brought the discussion to a close.

Yet Howard often brought fish next door to Grandma, and one afternoon he carried some fillets to Olga Engqvist, who profusely thanked him. "You know, Howard," she said, as he was about to leave, "I'd like to fish with you sometime. I used to go with Earl now and again, but I haven't fished even once since he died."

This request did not please my uncle. He told her that the water sometimes got rough, and, if anything should happen, he didn't know if he could keep her afloat.

"I've thought of that," she said. "What I'd really enjoy would be a day of ice fishing next winter." She smiled. "It used to be so cozy in Earl's old fish house. We'd play whist and eat chili and crackers. We'd heat coffee on the stove and bring donuts up from Johanson's Bakery. My, but we had lovely times."

Howard softened upon hearing the menu and agreed to find a day to take Olga along.

Meanwhile, he continued his summer bragging about the big ones he caught and the bigger ones that got away, and about the time a large northern came up and swallowed a baby duckling off Bear Island. "You do go on," Mother gently chided.

"Just upholding tradition," he said with a wink.

Howard no doubt figured Olga would forget about ice fishing, but right after Christmas she called him and reminded him of his promise. He said he'd try to arrange something.

But Olga didn't want to be the only woman on the ice, so she tried to convince Hilma to accompany her.

I was about twelve then, dropping off Grandma's grocery order, which I'd picked up at Paulson's Corner Market, and I overheard Olga and Hilma's discussion about the fishing trip. Olga, sitting at the kitchen table, sucked coffee through a sugar cube and told Hilma about the joys of fishing through a hole in the ice in the dead of a Duluth winter.

Hilma thought the whole matter ridiculous. "Ven I vas a girl up to Deerwood, ve used to fish because ve needed food. But to yust go out and freeze yewrself half to det . . . vy, Olga? Yew're a bigger fool dan I tot."

But Olga persisted as she dunked cookies and crumbed her coffee. "Hilma . . . we've been neighbors for forty years, and in all that time, you've never had an adventure."

"Yah? Who vas it vas cornered by da bear? Yew call dat no adwenture? Leaf da men do da fishing. I don't vant to do no fishing trew da ice."

"We'll have a grand time," said Olga. "We'll bring a nice pot of stew, and there's always fresh coffee. And should you catch a fish, why you'd just drop your teeth from excitement."

"Vat ewer gave yew da idea I vant to catch a fish anyvay, Olga?"

"I have a little philosophy, Hilma. I believe a person has to have new experiences in order to really be alive. Why, you're becoming nothing but an old fuddy-duddy." Olga coughed, then gentled her approach. "Well, I'd really enjoy your company, Hilma. And we'd only be gone a few hours."

Hilma wouldn't commit herself, and, over the next several days, Mrs. Engqvist kept at her. Finally, surprisingly, Hilma relented.

At the same time, Howard asked me to go along with him in case the ladies needed extra attention. "I can't imagine anything worse than being alone out on the ice with those two biddies," he said.

We set Saturday morning for the big outing. Howard had arranged for a four-person house out on Fish Lake, about fifteen miles from town. Olga awaited the day with great anticipation. She came over to Grandma's on Thursday in her ice-fishing attire. The clothing, which had belonged to Earl, was sizes too big. She wore a plaid wool shirt and a pair of wool navy dungarees with the thirteen-button front flap—a relic from Earl's World War I duty. The clothes reeked of moth balls. She also had a red-and-black-checked deerstalker cap, and she carried Earl's old navy pea coat, which dwarfed her, but would, she insisted, keep her warm as toast. She also had brought extra clothes that Hilma might like to wear.

"I ain't so big as yew, Olga," Hilma said diplomatically. "None of dat stuff vould fit me. I guess maybe I von't go. Nutting to vear."

"I bet some of Mom's clothes would fit you," I offered, squelching her excuse.

"I vouldn't bodder yewr mudder for her tings."

"No bother. I'll get you a nifty outfit for the day."

Finally dressed in borrowed clothes, Hilma did look a bit odd, but no more so than any other sixty-something woman who might do battle with wintry elements. She wore wool slacks over long underwear, two heavy sweaters, an old baseball jacket of mine, and two thick scarves about her head.

We departed at seven a.m. Saturday and headed out the Miller Trunk Highway. Howard seemed sullen, and the ladies were unusually quiet, until a terrible thought crossed Hilma's mind. "I knew dere vas someting vy I shouldn't go vit yew," she cried suddenly. "Vere does a person go to da batroom? Dey don't have no toilets in da middle of da lake."

Howard chuckled. "Why, you have to fend for yourself, Auntie. Adam and Eve didn't have plumbing either. They just went in the woods."

"Vell, sure, if yew got voods, dat's fine and dandy. But yew don't got no voods, no toilet paper, nutting. I'd burst before I vent out on da ice."

Olga giggled. "Let's cross that bridge if we get to it, Hilma. If worse comes to worse, you can always ask the men to look the other way."

"Somebody has tew tink about it," said Hilma.

"Well, so long as you only think about it, Hilma, you'll be fine."

Finally we arrived at the lake, and Howard drove out onto the ice to a fish house about a half mile from shore. The house was a relatively spacious affair with a small, home-made barrel stove against one wall and a card table in the middle. Four five-gallon paint containers turned upside down provided seating.

Howard brought in a box of scrap lumber and started the fire; I began chiseling out holes in each corner of the house, and Mrs. Engqvist started coffee from lake water.

Soon the fire crackled, and the ladies were seated. Howard and I rigged up the lines, impaling sucker minnows on number two hooks and dropping them into the holes. We wound extra line around cheap fly rod reels attached to short rods. Then Howard instructed the women. "Whenever you see your bobber disappear, count to ten and give a hard yank on the line to set the hook." He demonstrated. "Be sure you count to ten, or the fish will spit out the hook, and you'll lose him." He took his position at his spot and drew on his flask containing schnapps. "A quarter for the first fish," he added.

"Ve ain't going tew gamble, Howard," Hilma said.

"Pardon me, Howard," said Olga, "but how fast should we count to ten?"

Howard groaned. "Oh, take about a second for each count."

"Then I guess I should yank the line right now," she said.

"Not now, Olga. Good heavens, we just got here. I hope you ladies aren't—"

"Well, Howard, that bobber disappeared just as soon as you dropped it in the hole," Mrs. Engqvist said. And, indeed, line peeled off the crude reel she held in her mittened hand.

"Jerk the line!" I hollered. "Looks like a monster!"

Mrs. Engqvist reared back and set the hook, in the process falling off her seat.

Howard moved to aid her. She held tightly to the line, but it still slipped between her fingers. "Careful now, Olga, play him real easy," he said. "Don't let him bust the line."

"My, is this ever exciting," said Mrs. Engqvist. "Is this ever fun." She drew herself up on one knee.

Suddenly, the line slackened. "Oh-oh . . . he's off," Howard said. But, detecting movement in the line, he shouted, "Tighten her up. Quick."

He began helping Olga take up the slack. The two of them hastily grabbed loose line, dropping it behind them as the fish dashed back toward the hole. About thirty yards of loose line lay in swirls on the floor of the ice house. "He's running again," Howard hollered. "Give him line."

The fish continued forceful runs out for fifteen or twenty yards, then circled back. Line passed from Howard to Olga and back again, depending where the great fish surged. Howard was perspiring, and Olga became grim-faced, on her knees, peering into the dark hole. "If Earl could see this, Howard. This is really something."

"I just hope we can hold him, Olga," Howard said, shaking loose line from his fingers.

"Vun—tew—tree—" Hilma counted, staring into her hole. Her line too peeled off the reel. I grabbed it and yanked, setting the hook into something solid. Then I handed her the line. "Take him in, Hilma."

"Ooooh, he's heaby," Hilma said. With jaws clamped, she made small aspirate grunts with each heave on the line.

"Jeez, Olga, he feels heavier now than before," Howard gasped, as my bobber disappeared. I set the hook and also felt the pull of a strong fish. At the same moment, Hilma slipped and dropped her reel into the hole.

"Nuts," she exclaimed. "I lost da whole vorks."

"Sorry, Hilma," Howard yelled. "We got all we can handle here."

Hilma shrugged, stepped toward Howard's hole and stopped. "Eweryting's going hayvire," she said. "Now yewr bobber is gone tew, Howard."

"Dammit!" Howard cried. "Hold on here, Olga." He dashed for his own hole.

I continued wrestling with my line and saw Hilma's bobber pass beneath my hole. As I drew in my line, her bobber followed. I grabbed it and worked both lines. It suddenly occurred to me that there might be just one fish which had entangled all our lines.

A give-and-take battle seesawed another five minutes, with the line laying in knotted, twisted coils like trim black snakes at our feet. Howard was losing heart, realizing that the mess would never unravel even if the fish were landed. It seemed fruitless.

Hilma, moving to the stove for the coffee pot, became snared in the line and fell against the wall, knocking the chimney connection from the stove. The house quickly filled with smoke. I kicked open the door to let the smoke escape, but all of us coughed, engulfed by acrid fumes. "Endure, friends, endure," cried Mrs. Engqvist. "Hold a damp hankie to your faces." She wasn't about to let that fish go.

"Dere's no hankies here, Olga," snapped Hilma. "Ve don't ewen have toilet paper." She floundered toward the door as the fish made one monumental lunge. And, with that rush, tangled line around the legs of the card table, upending it, sending the coffee pot and stew kettle crashing and splattering the back of Olga's deerstalker with bits of cabbage and carrot. As the fish resumed his surge, the table spun into the stove, and the house started on fire.

"Isn't dis a pickle," Hilma yelped.

"Abandon ship," called Mrs. Engqvist, and we all scrambled outside as flames licked the wooden walls of the ice house.

From a house ten yards distant, a fisherman burst out and ran toward us, oblivious of our predicament. "You'll never believe this," he shouted. "I was fishing there and all of a sudden, I see three . . . four bobbers come swooping by, and then my line is hit, and I lost the whole rig. Must have been a world record northern." He leaned over and pressed his mittened thumb against one nostril and snirted.

Hilma turned away in disgust.

"Never seen nothing like that before," said the fisherman,

who finally noticed our fire. "What in the world happened here?"

"Fish," Howard said dejectedly.

"Fish? What do you mean, fish?"

"Mister, you wouldn't believe it anyway," said Olga.

She was no doubt right. Almost nobody else did either, which was of great consternation to Hilma, who told many of her acquaintances at work and friends from church about her experience. "Dey yust don't believe me," she complained several days later. "Dey hewt and howl. And Mrs. Grandahl yust out and says, 'Hilma, yew're a liar.' Imagine—calling me a liar."

Howard smiled kindly and put his hand on her shoulder. "Now you know what all us fishermen go through," he told her. "If I was to take you down to the Friendly Tavern and have you tell that story, nobody'd call you a liar, Hilma. They'd just say, 'That old lady's a real fisherman.'"

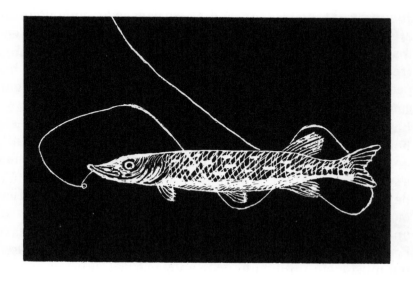

10

M. Johanson's Twists

During my pre-adolescence, the twists baked by M. Johanson at the M. Johanson Bakery earned legendary status among pupils at Grant Elementary School in Duluth's Central Hillside neighborhood. All the Scandinavians, especially, frequented the bakery, and Aunt Hilma was quite fond of his peanut butter cookies. Grandma only made ginger and sugar cookies.

M—I never did learn his name—baked bread and sweets in the basement beneath his home on the corner of Seventh Avenue East and Tenth Street—kitty corner from Nathan Horowitz' Grocery.

The twists consisted of nothing more than deep fat-fried strands of braided dough liberally rolled in sugar. But to hundreds of Grant kids they were mouthfuls of heaven.

M resembled an old-country artisan with a large drooping mustache. With white hair and perpetually covered with flour dust, he had a chalky, almost apparition-like appearance. When he wandered outside, he sometimes left flour footprints on the sidewalk for several yards as he ambled down the street. Tiny particles of flour dust continually fell from his large, hairy hands and light blue work shirt.

The neighborhood children never gave a thought to his breads—large, crusty loaves baked with gray, unbleached flour, or his heavy peanut butter cookies. We were interested only in the twists, which he sold two for a nickel.

If I ate two twists, I stayed full through supper. Whenever I complained of a waning appetite at dinner, Mom inevitably accused, "You ate twists after school, didn't you?" Sometimes she was right.

If truth be known, however, I was never all that excited about the twists. The best thing about them was the price. A nickel, no everyday commodity among my peers, was a treasure, a rare treat from a parent, or a prize for winning a bicycle race at the Central Field Playground track, or for memorizing ten Bible verses in Sunday School class. A nickel would buy one candy bar, one popsicle, one bottle of soda pop, but *two* relatively large twists.

I ate them because everyone else did too, though "ate" is the polite term. "Wolfed" is more appropriate. When one of our mates would try to sneak away with a nickel and buy two fresh twists, we would waylay him on the street and cajole him into sharing. Failing that, we fought him; one held him down while another wrenched the brown bag from him and took the larger of the two twists. Which was only right. A young lad should never have been allowed to eat two giant twists by himself.

I should have gotten a clear inkling into the substance of those twists early on. The small brown paper sack into which Mr. Johanson dropped the twists would be saturated with grease before one walked a dozen steps away from his shop. And many was the time, when wrestling over a bag of them, we'd wind up with large grease stains on school shirts.

One time, in the midst of a scuffle for a twist purchased by Googins Gernander, the bag was squashed on my best pair of brown oxfords. The stain remained on the shoe for as long as I wore it. When Mother asked what the stain was, I explained, "Somebody squashed a twist on it."

"Gee whiz," she moaned. "And to think you kids eat those things. Don't come crying to me with your next stomach ache, if you've been eating those twists."

The fat-sodden twists were the forerunner of the contemporary sinkers—leaden donuts that when dunked in a cup of coffee immediately plummeted to the bottom. M. Johanson's twists were heavy, and sometimes small children, carrying two in a sack, seemed to tilt leeward as they walked.

Still, I gobbled them after school whenever a stray nickel fell into my hands. I broke my addiction, however, one summer afternoon while I biked alone. Pedalling around the neighborhood and searching vainly for playmates, I wandered back toward Grant School and surveyed the vacant playground, then continued west another block. No one was in front of Horowitz's Grocery—a traditional gathering spot for kids. However, my olfactory senses were assaulted by the odors from the bakery. I had a nickel that I had planned to spend on a cherry popsicle later that afternoon, but the lure of the bakery and M's twists was too strong.

I could purchase two twists and eat them myself without having to share. I could eat them slowly, savoring the sweet, doughy texture, and licking the sugar granules from my fingers. Suddenly, being alone in the middle of a summer afternoon was a godsend. Two twists to be devoured with no one else demanding to share.

I dragged my bike down the steps and laid it on the grass just off the sidewalk leading to the bakery. I took no risks; if perchance an acquaintance came along and recognized my bike, he'd hit me up for one of my pastries. Down on the grass, my bike wouldn't be visible from the street above.

I went inside. The bakery was dimly lit, and the bread on cooling racks behind the small glass display case was gray and flour-dusty, like M. Johanson himself. There were some chocolate cupcakes in the case, and a few glazed donuts, a couple of Danish, and perhaps three or four twists lying on white, oil-stained paper. Mr. Johanson reached for a small brown bag and snapped it open. "Well, sonny," he said without expression, "twists?"

I nodded. He reached into the case and grabbed two, dropping them into the sack. He crimped it once, then handed it to me. I surrendered my nickel and started for the door. Emerging from the darkened bakery, I squinted into the August sunshine and jammed the first twist into my mouth. I chewed two or three times, then swallowed. There remained but one bite of the first twist. My vision cleared; I was in luck. No one was around. I popped the second mouthful, chewed and swallowed. The second twist I would eat more slowly as I rode my bike.

My fingers slipped from the handlebars as I attempted to right the old Schwinn, and I discovered that my hands were shiny from the twist grease. The brown bag was darkening fast, so I removed the second twist and tossed the bag away. A small white dog leaped on it and began tearing into it. I pushed my bike up the steps and started pedalling east on Tenth Street. Happily, I took a smaller bite of the second twist. I solemnly chewed and tasted. I swallowed. The substance left a slick residue inside my mouth. My belly felt heavy. I cleared my throat and spat. I didn't feel so good. I examined what remained of the twist in my left hand. A trickle of grease had descended below my wrist. I dropped the twist in the middle of Tenth Street and drove my bike over it. It seemed to squish like an over-ripe pear, leaving a grease smear the size of a volleyball encircling the flattened pastry.

I knew I could never again eat a twist, and thought the matter would be forgotten until one afternoon a month later, after school had resumed. A friend invited me to join him in a twist as we walked toward our school patrol stations. I declined, but, since he was a friend, I wished to share with him my revelation about the twists. I directed his attention to a fading splotch in the middle of Tenth Street. "What do you think that is?" I asked, pointing.

"Somebody's car leaked oil," he said.

"I ran over a twist last month," I said. "The grease is still there."

He recoiled. "Grease?" he said, stretching out the word. Then he shuddered.

Over the next couple of days, other kids congregated and examined the smear in the street. Several years later my brother David, four years younger than I, said he'd never heard of twists, and nobody he knew went to M. Johanson's Bakery.

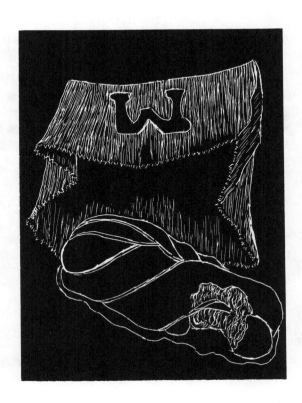

11

The Exorcism

Though Emmaline Walsh was not a resident of our old neighborhood, during the summer of 1952 she made a major impact on Olga Engqvist.

Mrs. Walsh, a stout woman with the continually dour mien of an Irish washerwoman, had been regularly employed as a cleaner and launderer by Avril Steppe, who lived next door, south of us. Mrs. Walsh hoped to expand her clientele in the neighborhood even though few residents employed cleaning ladies. She spent Wednesdays at Mrs. Steppe's, and, after a dozen or so visits, she arrived on the block to knock on doors and offer her services to other wives. Actually she did more than offer; her approach was almost insistent.

After perhaps thirty minutes with Mother, she wheedled a tryout. Mother, vexed at having given in, at one point asked me how she would tell Mrs. Walsh she really wasn't needed.

"Just tell her," I said, with a thirteen-year-old's impatient wisdom.

"That's easier said than done," Mother said. "Your father

71

will be furious."

"That's why you have to tell her."

Mrs. Walsh managed to complete the chores within three hours, and Mother rewarded her with five or six dollars, saying, "Your work is awfully good, and I wouldn't hesitate to recommend you to anyone who needs cleaning. But right now, I really don't think we'll be needing that extra help. I have two boys big enough to help out around here."

"Well," Mrs. Walsh started slowly, counting out the one-dollar bills Mother had given her, "you got that baby here too, Missus, and I think you *could* use the help. I had five boys of me own to raise, and they wasn't no picnic, I can tell you. But, I don't want to be no bother. So anyway, thank you, Missus."

The next week she was at Grandma's house when I came to read the morning sports pages. Grandma insisted that she required no help, but invited Mrs. Walsh to have coffee. Seated at Grandma's kitchen table, Mrs. Walsh consumed perhaps ten ginger cookies and two or three date bars. And while thoroughly dominating the conversation, espoused her theories about ordinary house dust causing explosive fires that could nearly melt a grown man. She'd seen it happen more than once—dozens of times, in fact. She went on at some length too about how rats and mice loved those dirty corners in kitchens. She scanned Grandma's spotless kitchen, frowning fiercely as her gaze riveted on the corners. "Basements is good for rats and mice too, you know. Most folks don't bother to give the basement much attention until it's too late. I don't mind giving a basement a good scrubbing myself, but that's the way I am."

Hilma stolidly said nothing during the conversation, while Grandma merely nodded or said, "My, my," to Mrs. Walsh's pronouncements.

After about an hour, Mrs. Walsh left to try her luck with Olga Engqvist, in the corner house on Tenth Avenue East and Tenth Street.

"Dat vun vill hit it fine vit Olga," Hilma said. "Dey bote got crasy ideas. And if she ain't careful, she'll be fat as a gewse. She gobbled up dat whole plate of cookies."

"I was pleased she enjoyed them," Grandma said. "Poor soul."

"Yew can't alvays let dem take yew for a fool, Gustie," said Hilma. "Yew've yust newer learned dat, have yew? Yew remember my fadder used to say how da servants vould yip folks and steal? Vell, it'll happen here yust da same as in Sveden."

I had by now finished the paper, and Grandma invited me for cookies and milk. "Mrs. Walsh didn't eat all of them," she said.

I bolted down three or four and teased Hilma about a story in the paper that said bears might be invading the city again that summer. She wasn't in the mood, however, and said, "I got no time for yewr teasing, Mickey."

She rose from the table but was interrupted on her way to the pantry by the sound of the front door opening. Olga Engqvist burst in without knocking. "Oh, Gustie . . . Hilma, I'm so glad you folks are at home."

"Yew could have knocked," Hilma intoned.

"I'm sorry, Hilma. I really should have."

"Is something wrong, Olga?" Grandma asked. "You're looking awfully upset."

Olga took the chair vacated by Hilma. She tightened the maroon scarf around her late husband's old fedora. "Was that woman here . . . Mrs. Walsh?"

"Yes, she stopped by," Grandma said. "But we don't need cleaning help. We told her. She seemed like a pleasant woman."

"My foot," huffed Hilma. "She like tew eat us out of house and home. And ve couldn't get a vord in etchvise."

Olga loosened the scarf beneath her chin. "Well, I don't know quite what to make of her, but she wasn't in the house two minutes and she tells me she senses a presence."

"Vell, yew vasn't going to give her no present, Olga," Hilma said. "Yew don't ewen know her. Dat takes real nerve, if yew ask me." Hilma crossed her arms.

"She did strike me as a bold woman," said Grandma. "But who would imagine her thinking a total stranger would give her a present?"

"No, no . . . you don't understand," Olga said. "My goodness, she says my house is possessed."

"Vell, of course it's possessed," Hilma said. "Yew possess it, Olga. Earl paid gewd money for dat house, and yew've possessed it for many years now."

"I'm afraid you still don't understand, Hilma. Mrs. Walsh says my house has some nasty spirits in it. She thinks it might have been someone who lived there before—many years ago. She says the spirit is unhappy and wants me out of the house."

"Spirit?" Hilma set her jaws. "Vell, I should say. Yew keep dat voman avay from yewr house and eweryting vill be yust fine, Olga. Da idea."

"You know," began Olga, a bit calmer now, "I used to love to read ghost stories when I was a youngster about Mickey's age." She removed her scarf and hat. "Oh, my, how they'd give me a fright. But I never thought there was any such thing, not really. And now this woman comes and tells me such a thing. She says she couldn't work in the house even if I hired her. She said I'd need to exorcise the house."

"Exercise? How do you exercise a house?" I asked, chuckling.

My interjection received no response, and Mrs. Engqvist continued. "She might be right, you know. I mean things have seemed funny lately."

"Den yew're as nuts as she is," Hilma asserted.

"Olga, you really ought to know better," said Grandma, filling her cup with the boiling hot water she drank in lieu of coffee or tea, which were forbidden her by her doctor. "I've been in that house a thousand times, and we both know there's not a thing wrong with that house."

"Mrs. Walsh says she could make the spirit leave," Olga said weakly.

"Sure, and take yew for ewery dime yew got," Hilma said.

Olga sighed. "You just never know these days. Strange things happening all over. I just don't feel safe now."

"Uff," grunted Hilma. "Olga, I don't vant to hear no more of dis foolishness. Yew got a mind of yewr own and yew know vat's vat. Bote yew and Gustie are tew qvick to trust folks vit crasy notions."

By now Olga sensed that there was little sympathy for her predicament, so she briefly directed the conversation toward the mundane for a few moments, then left. I departed with her, and, once we were onto the front porch, I asked if she really believed in ghosts.

"Well, Mickey, that's part of the problem. I don't know. I don't want to, but I read so many ghost stories when I was younger, I think maybe I do in a way." She looked at me and touched my arm. "You don't think I'm nuts do you, Mickey?"

"Not usually," I said, teasing.

She forced a half smile. "Oh, yes you do. I know you kids, and you all think I'm looney."

I didn't respond immediately, and she went on. "May I ask a favor, Mickey?"

"Sure."

"Would you come over to the house with me? I'd feel better if there was someone there with me. I'm going to call Mrs. Miller to come over, but if you stay with me until she gets here in just a few minutes, I'd really appreciate it."

"All right," I said reluctantly. I was apprehensive myself, but at least it was daylight. "Maybe you should have Mrs. Walsh get rid of the spirits like you said."

She clapped me on the shoulder. "That's the stuff I've been waiting to hear, Mickey," she said. "You got a good head on your shoulders."

We started across Grandma's lawn to Mrs. Engqvist's

house. "Do you know how they get rid of spirits in houses?" I asked.

"No, I don't. If I did, I would run them off myself. I suppose there's a lot of rigamarole involved. Let's see if she's still at Mrs. Steppe's house and have her come right over to do it. You've saved my day, Mickey."

"Wasn't anything special," I said.

A bumblebee swept into her house with us as she held open the screen door for me to enter first. I hesitated before stepping inside the front parlor. I had heard that rooms were cool in the presence of ghosts, and now I really felt uneasy. It *was* cold in Olga's house. The shades were drawn and the room darkened. "Maybe you should pull up the shades," I offered.

"That's the second good idea you've had today, Mickey," she said and raised the blinds, allowing the morning light to bathe the room and its deep, soft chairs and sofas.

The phone sat on a small stand by the stairs leading to the second floor. Mrs. Engqvist looked up Avril Steppe's phone number and called. Mrs. Walsh said she'd be right over.

"Well, that's that," said Olga. "Now, perhaps you'll take some tea."

"I don't like tea," I said.

She eyed me. "Well, if you must know, I don't much either. But in all those silly ghost stories I read, folks were always drinking tea. It seems appropriate, so I'm going to have some anyway. I'll bet Mrs. Walsh will enjoy a cup too."

I closely followed her into the kitchen. She drew water and set the kettle on to boil. She placed two cups on the table and dropped a tea bag into each one. Before the water had begun to boil, Mrs. Walsh was at the door.

Mrs. Engqvist let her in and pointed to me. "I suppose you've met my young friend Mickey. He's just the best of boys. I tell you I don't know what we'd do around here without him. Of course, his whole family is just tops. You can't beat them."

Mrs. Walsh nodded grimly. "Yes, I suppose so," she said.

"You'll have a cup of tea?" Mrs. Engqvist asked.

"Never touch the stuff."

"Well then, I won't have any either. I just thought . . . oh, well. Should I do anything?"

"You wouldn't know how, Missus. I can take care of this in no time." She placed her cloth bag on a chair and took off her coat. She pushed back the sleeves of her housedress and nodded at Mrs. Engqvist and me.

"Where do you want us then, Mrs. Walsh?" Olga asked.

"Makes no nevermind to me," she said. "I'll just get busy here in the front room." She walked toward the front door, then turned around, clapped her hands together twice and made a shooing movement with them. "Be gone—be gone," she said flatly. Then she picked up her bag, grabbed a hankie and blew her nose.

Mrs. Engqvist and I stared. Mrs. Walsh noticed us. "Do you have any food handy?"

"Well, I suppose I could make a quick meatloaf sandwich," Olga said, puzzled.

"That would be all right," Mrs. Walsh said. "Try to hurry." She followed Mrs. Engqvist into the kitchen and sat at the table. "It's so dark and cold in this house," she said.

"Isn't that from the spirits?" Mrs. Engqvist asked.

"I really couldn't say," said Mrs. Walsh.

Mrs. Engqvist placed a slice of cold meatloaf on white bread and handed it to Mrs. Walsh.

"Catsup and mustard," ordered Mrs. Walsh.

Mrs. Engqvist produced them, and the cleaning lady liberally doused the meat with the condiments before taking a huge bite, chewing rapidly, then swallowing. She devoured the sandwich in three or four bites. "You don't have anything to drink, I don't suppose?"

"I was about to make tea before you came," Olga said.

"I already said, no tea. Don't like it."

"Well, there's some orangeade we made last night."

"Good. Good."

Mrs. Engqvist poured a tall glass, which Mrs. Walsh tossed down in two long gulps. She wiped her mouth with her hands, then put her coat on. "I won't charge you for this, Missus," she said. "But if you need some cleaning help, I sure hope you remember me." She started for the door.

"Um, is that all?" asked Olga.

"Well, they're gone now. So I'll be running along." She burped and opened the front door, lumbering heavily across the porch and down the front steps. She waddled out toward the sidewalk and was gone.

"Well, can you beat that?" Olga said after a long pregnant pause. "I think I've been hoodwinked by all this hocus-pocus. Your Aunt Hilma was right, I'm afraid. That woman is goofy."

Uncle Howard found out about Mrs. Walsh the next day and was enormously amused with the exorcism. "And all she said was, 'Be gone—be gone'?" he repeated, doubling over with laughter. "Be gone—that was it?"

"I swear to you, Howard, that's all she did," said Mrs. Engqvist.

As for Mrs. Walsh, her attempts to secure more cleaning jobs in our neighborhood went for naught. Not long after, she made the mistake of knocking on Bert Carlson's door. As soon as he saw her, he burst out laughing. "Be gone—be gone," he said. "Be gone."

12

The Unmaking of a Missionary

Later that year, in mid-November, I had slept late on a Saturday morning and didn't make it next door to peruse the sports section until nearly noon. I'd barely cracked the pages when Hilma came into the kitchen, waving an envelope at me and smiling. "Got a letter tewday from Reuben," she announced brightly.

I was not much interested in the missive from Reuben, a missionary our church sponsored in Siam. Hilma took all of life seriously but nothing more so than her religion. She belonged to the Swedish Baptist Church, making her an outsider among others of her predominantly Lutheran nationality. Hilma regarded Lutherans as an apostate lot, charging that Lutherans had cheated her father out of his considerable holdings near Bergen, Sweden, forcing the family to immigrate in ignominious penury to this country in 1887.

Having never married, her church became her passion. She received letters from Reuben because she faithfully mailed him a five-dollar check each month from her own meager earnings as a seamstress. Beyond this, however, she always insisted that *I* become a missionary too. She inevitably read Reuben's letters to me shortly after they arrived, encouraging me to emulate the sainted Reuben.

As usual I tried concentrating on the sports pages while she read, making appropriate listening noises whenever she paused. I looked up when her pause lengthened. She folded the letter in her lap. "Vouldn't it be vunderful," she said, beaming, her eyes moist behind her trifocals, "if vun day yew could be a missionary ower in Siam vit Reuben?"

I nodded dully, and she went on about the seminary in St. Paul I'd attend, reminding me that cousin Jimmy went there and was a pastor in Phoenix. "Jimmy is a real minister too," she said. "But dat's nutting compared to a missionary who vorks vit da headens in da yungles."

It wasn't my intention to work with jungle heathens, but I couldn't tell that to my great aunt. Instead, she discovered that by herself the next day.

I attended her church with my mother and younger brothers, but rarely sat with them or with Aunt Hilma during services. Instead I sat with my friend, David Strom, and with a thirtyish man named Max, who was a spastic. Max's body and face were twisted and his speech somewhat slurred, but he was readily accepted by younger kids in the congregation. He possessed a keen mind and was an excellent chess player. His sense of humor, however, was sophomoric, which explained his appeal to David and me. He used to tell us slightly ribald jokes during sermons, sending us dashing from the sanctuary stifling giggles, while we drew stern stares from adults.

In time we moved our seating to the balcony, a haunt usually reserved for parents with young children who might require nursery tending. The church nursery was attached behind the balcony. But since several volunteers tended the nursery, parents most often returned downstairs, leaving the balcony nearly vacant, except for young boys bent on fractious behavior.

The balcony was not a perfect retreat, though, as a city police officer, also a church member, usually sat there too, managing to maintain a semblance of order. We suspected he felt sorry for Max, for he was reluctant to admonish him for loud whispering or talking.

Services at church normally ended about noon, with the congregation growing restless whenever the pastor's sermon overran that hour.

But that next Sunday, while our minister was out of town, a visiting evangelist took his place. It became apparent to all in attendance that, as the noon hour approached, the evangelist wasn't winding down, but was, in fact, just getting started. At 12:15 he said, "I know I'm running a bit long this morning, but the Lord has laid a burden on my heart. . . ."

Ten minutes later he asked us to please bear with him a few more minutes. At 12:30 he repeated his plea and continued fervently. At 12:55 he raised his arms. "Oh, people, do you hear me?" his voice crescendoed. "Do you hear the message this morning?"

Max, his face hot with anger and frustration, stood in the second row of the balcony. "Ah, bullshit," he bellowed, then stalked out of the balcony and clomped down the stairs.

David and I crimsoned and slipped down the back stairs where Max was zipping his jacket near the cloak room. A few other adults began retrieving their coats and boots, offering weak, embarrassed smiles. "My pork roast is about to burn," said one woman, as she picked up a camel-colored coat. "But wasn't his message thrilling?"

"You must be nuts," Max snarled.

David and I had stifled ourselves too long by then, and we began to laugh as the woman departed. We clutched thick wool coat sleeves and stuffed them into our mouths so our eruptions wouldn't be heard in the sanctuary. I slid to the floor, tears coursing down my cheeks. David suddenly sobered, held his belly, snorted another laugh and began to retch. He grabbed a large, man's overshoe and vomited.

I pounded the floor limply, my abdomen in spasms. David, still hunched over the boot, and I heard the organ strike the opening chords of "The Doxology." I scrambled to my feet and tugged at David. "We got to get out of here," I said.

We made it into the foyer and down the stairs into the men's room, where David took a long drink, and I splashed water on my face and cleared my throat. I started giggling again, and David grabbed me.

"Don't. I'm sick. I can't take any more."

We went upstairs then. The cloak room filled with parishioners struggling into wraps and boots. While searching for my own coat, I saw a man slip into the "overshoe." There was a suctiony, gurgling sound as his booted foot contacted the floor.

"Well, what in the world?" he murmured, extracting the offended shoe from the boot. "What's this? What in the world is this?" he asked of no one in particular.

"Golly, I hope it isn't what I think it is," a woman said, wrinkling her nose.

"Well, who would do a thing like this?" the man asked as he carefully kicked off the shoe and worked his sock loose. "My goodness, I'm a mess."

This was too much for me, and I dashed outside and pressed a handful of snow against my head to keep from laughing again. David slumped against the side of his father's station wagon and held his sides.

Seated around Grandma's Sunday dinner table an hour or so later, Hilma announced, "I know someting, and I'm ashamed."

My father, who seldom attended church, looked absently at her. "What would that be?"

"Some boys made a commotion at church dis morning."

"Shush, Hilma," said Grandma, who didn't like the tone of Hilma's voice.

"I von't shush, Gustie," she said. "I von't shush, ewen dough I'm ashamed."

"If you're going to tell us about Mickey throwing up in Abner Swanson's boot this morning, forget it," Uncle Howard said. "Nobody needs to know a thing like that at the dinner table."

"What?" my mother said, dropping her salad fork in her coffee cup.

"I didn't throw up," I said. "David Strom did. And what was he supposed to do, vomit on the floor?"

"Uff—Mickey," said Aunt Hilma, shaking her head. "Maybe yew shouldn't be tinking about being a missionary. At least not for a vile yet. Vat sort of headen vould listen to a missionary who goes to church and womits in anodder man's owershoe?"

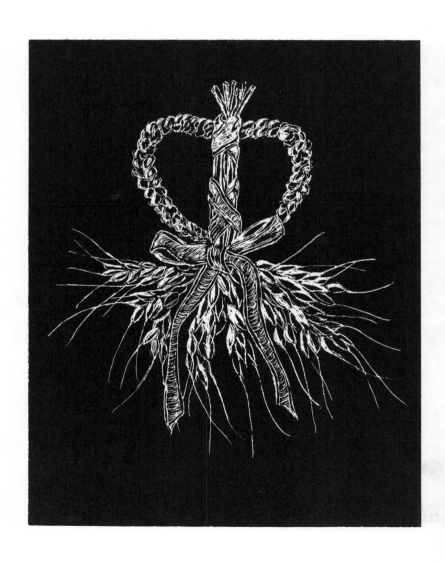

13

Christmas 1953

My Grandma Norquist had always been tenderhearted. During the first days of the Depression, she provided board and occasionally bed for down-and-out panhandlers and drifters. Even when I was a small boy, some of the drifters routinely walked several miles from the rail yards to knock on her door at 924 Tenth Avenue East. She never turned any-one away hungry. And there were times when I would drop in to her house in the middle of the afternoon to see a strange, shabbily-dressed man eating a substantial meal.

Such men visited perhaps four or five times a year, and they didn't get hastily thrown together leftovers either. Grandma might fix meatballs or Spanish rice; perhaps mashed potatoes, gravy, dark home-baked bread, and plenty of coffee.

As her special gift to the indigent at Christmas in 1953, she decided to invite two men from the bowery Bethel House to share our Christmas Eve meal. "We have so much," she told David and me, who were none too pleased with the intrusion into our tradition.

On the morning of the twenty-fourth, I woke early when mother entered my bedroom and tore the covers off me. "You have to get up now," she said. "I need your help right away." She tried to pull me from the bed. "Come on. Up. We've lots to do."

"Like what?" I snapped, rolling free of her grasp.

"Your father's gone to get a tree, and we have a whole string of lights that are shot. You have to go down to the Glass Block and get some new ones. They're on sale. Now hurry. I've got all kinds of baking to do, and Stevie is downstairs crying over his breakfast."

Stephen, my youngest brother, who came along twelve years after me and eight after David, was two years old and indeed wailed from the kitchen below.

"Please hurry," Mother said, leaving my room. "Don't make me call you again."

Downstairs, Steve continued to whimper. The house was redolent of carbon, and wafts of smoke floated into the hallway. "Darn," Mother cried. "I've burned the cookies!" I entered the kitchen to see Mom removing a tray of smoking spritz cookies.

"Cookie!" wailed Steve, and the phone rang.

It was Aunt Ada, who wanted to speak to Mother.

"Take a message," Mom ordered, scraping the charred ruins into the garbage.

I had recently seen Al Kelly, the double-talk artist on a Candid Camera segment, and had been much taken with him. Suddenly, wickedly, I decided to try double-talk myself. "She can't creen with golfungs now, Ada. She's got these brudnorks in her sklang. Maybe you should call back in a little while." I hung up.

Mom was still scraping the cookie tin when Steve dumped the oatmeal he no longer wanted over his head. Mom moaned, and the phone rang again. Ada had called back. "Is something wrong with Mona?" she asked.

"You better talk to her yourself," I said, grinning. "It's those crutchnorgs again." I turned to Mother, who was trying to pry open a window to let out the smoke. "It's for you, Mom."

"Take care of Stephen," she said, grabbing the phone. Steve's oatmeal ran down his face. It matted his hair.

I went to the sink to clean him up and handed him a plastic bottle of Lux dish soap to occupy him while I scrubbed his face and hair. Mom, meanwhile, was wondering what in the world Ada gibbered about. Steve continued to fuss. I cast a sidelong glance at Mom, then raised the Lux to Steve's lips and gave him a squirt. He swallowed several times, made a face, and expelled pink suds from his mouth, which ran down his jersey and puddled on the floor.

Mother hung up the phone and rushed for him. "What's wrong? What did you do to him?"

"He ate some soap," I said, pointing to the bottle.

"Oooooh, that's all I need," she groaned, rushing Steve to the sink and holding him over it.

"At least he isn't whining anymore," I offered, then grabbed my jacket and dashed down to Ninth Street to catch a downtown bus.

Superior Street was inordinately clogged with pedestrian and auto traffic, but I managed to slog my way through to the Glass Block department store, only to find it literally jammed to the revolving door with shoppers. Claustrophobic, I backed out and hit the street. Battling crowds everywhere, I slipped into the Granada Book Store for refuge, and there I broke the ten Mom had given me and purchased a comic book. Then I caught the East Eighth Street bus for home.

When I reached the house, Dad was there with the tree he'd purchased for a quarter at the Pure Oil station at Twelfth Avenue East and Ninth Street. Trees cost a dollar and up even then, but Dad, waiting until Christmas Eve, always managed to get a tree with what he called character, and what Mom called huge gaps between branches.

"Where are the lights?" Mom asked.

"It was too crowded there," I said. "I'd never have gotten through."

Her hands flew to her face, and she dissolved in tears. "We can't have a tree without lights," she sobbed.

"Didn't he get lights?" Dad bellowed from the living room.

"No," I replied timidly. "It was too crowded in the store."

"Dammit to hell anyway," Dad roared. "Whoever heard of a tree without lights? That's what makes the thing Christmas, for crying out loud."

David left the room crabbing about not having a proper tree to put presents under, while I sneaked next door to Grandma's.

Parked in front of Grandma's house was Uncle Howard's nifty 1950 Plymouth. Just a few weeks earlier, Bert Carlson loaned him $300, which he used to purchase the car.

"You want to go for a ride, Mickey?" he asked as I entered Grandma's fragrant kitchen.

"Sure," I said. Howard's was the latest model car on either side of the family. Dad still drove a 1949 Ford, and had grumbled about Howard being out of work and still having a better car than he himself could afford.

About 3:30 we got into Howard's new vehicle and headed up Tenth Avenue, turning west on Tenth Street, on our way to pick up the fellows from the Bethel Home. Howard accelerated, then hit a patch of ice. The car slid out of control as a black Nash backed out of an alleyway. Howard's Plymouth plowed into the rear end of it. I was jostled but unhurt. Howard slowly opened his door and, rubbing his jaw, eased out.

"You got the whole damn street to drive in, but you needed my spot too, hey, Mister?" an angry voice called from the other car. It was Bert's voice.

"Bert? That you? I hit some ice, Bert," Howard said, gingerly touching his forehead now. "Went into a skid and couldn't stop her."

Bert climbed out of his car. "Jeez, Howard, if I'da known you was gonna take my money to buy a car that you'd use to smash *my* car, you'da never got a dime."

"It was an accident, Bert. An accident. I'm banged up and everything here. Mickey, you okay?" he hollered as I stepped from the car. I nodded.

Howard turned to Bert again. "If you'da looked, you'da seen me coming."

"Well, who'd think some maniac would come barreling down the street on the ice and just plow into a car that was backing out? I'm minding my own business, Howard, till you come along."

Howard didn't respond, but limped around the wreckage, assessing the damages. "City crews shoulda been out sanding today," he muttered. "They think because it's Christmas Eve they can sit on their butts back in the garage and get soused."

"We called 'em yesterday," Bert said, "and told 'em they should get some sand down. But we ain't seen 'em nowhere."

"Jeez, lookit my car, Bert," Howard groaned.

"Your car—what about mine?"

Howard appeared crestfallen. His radiator leaked profusely, and the front of his car accordioned half-way to the windshield.

The DeSoto's rear end had fared better, and Bert reasoned his car was only minimally damaged. Taking pity on his friend, he said, "Aw, look, Howard, I know it wasn't your fault. It coulda happened to anybody. Come on in and we'll take a little nip to ease your pain."

I went back to Grandma's and told her about the accident, and said that, while no one was hurt, Howard had gone to Bert's for a drink. Howard's wife, Gwen, just shook her head. "I'm not surprised," she said quietly.

Grandma lowered her eyes and called Dad, asking if he would please pick up the men from the Bethel.

Dad changed clothes and barked orders to the rest of

the family to get the packages together and bring them over to Grandma's so everything would be ready by the time he got there.

When everyone arrived at Grandma's, the house familiarly smelled of the lutefisk which would be served with allspice and cream sauce. David tiptoed into the kitchen and came back smiling. "She's made two potato sausage rings," he whispered, having feared earlier that the bowery men wouldn't like lutefisk and would eat all of the sausage, forcing us to endure the lutefisk, which we abhorred.

Everyone, save Howard, sat in Grandma's living room when Dad arrived with the two guests. Grandma greeted the men warmly and introduced them. The bald man was Leon, and the other, a taller, thinner man with unkempt red hair and a scraggly beard, was Elwood. Their clothing was clean, but rumpled; bib overalls and sweatshirt on Leon, while Elwood wore a complete outfit of janitor's greens. Both men carried on their breaths the sour smell of that morning's muscatelle. Neither spoke when introduced, but their sunken cheeks indicated toothlessness.

"Where's Howard?" Dad asked, hanging up his coat.

"Getting drunk vit fat Bert," Hilma grunted.

"Should we wait for him?" Dad asked.

"It's Christmas," said Grandma. "He'll be along shortly."

"We sat uneasily silent in the living room, while Grandma, Mother, and Gwen puttered in the kitchen. Hilma knitted in her rocker. Ada placed candles on the table. Dad grabbed the morning paper and read. David and I squirmed in our chairs, while Leon and Elwood sat stolidly on the davenport. Finally Elwood asked Dad if he had a cigarette.

Briefly lowering his paper, Dad said, "No, sorry, Bud. Don't smoke." The paper went up. Elwood coughed a phlegmy cough.

The house grew tense with Howard's not coming. Finally Mother started bringing food to the table; the platter of lutefisk, looking like grey jello; the sausage rings; a large bowl of boiled potatoes; carrots and peas swimming in melted butter; fresh dinner rolls; a jello and fruit cocktail salad; and a large relish tray containing pickled beets and pickled onions that only Howard used to eat.

As we were about to go to the table, Howard came in. His face was brandy-reddened, and he stumbled over the throw rug in the entry. Leon and Elwood sat forward, recognizing a fellow in his cups.

Hilma was immediately disgusted with my uncle who attempted to plant a Christmas kiss on her cheek. "No kiss," she snapped, turning away. "Not ven yew've been drinking."

"Sorry I'm late folks," Howard said, speaking slowly, deliberately. "I had an accident out there this afternoon. Hit that ice there, and she just slammed into Bert's car. Fine Christmas, huh? I got hurt too. My jaw don't feel good at all, and I got a nasty bruise on my forehead. Here, have a look Mona," he said to Mother.

"We're sorry about your accident, Howard," Mother said coolly. "We've been waiting dinner for nearly an hour. Are you ready to eat now?"

"Yah. Sure. Lead me to it." He paused and indicated to the two guests to precede him. "After you, my friends," he slurred.

We sat, and David and I said grace—Come Lord Jesus— in rapid unison.

"Anybody here seen my car?" Howard asked, piling lutefisk and potatoes on his plate. "Wrecked, smashed to smithereens. Ruined."

Nobody responded, nor was there any other conversation, except hushed requests that food be passed. Neither Leon nor Elwood asked for additional helpings, though whenever Grandma suggested they take more food, they matched Howard in loading their plates. They ate quickly, gumming down great mouthfuls of lutefisk, sausage, potatoes and jello, daubing up cream sauce and butter with chunks of Grandma's rolls.

As the food began disappearing, Mother went to the kitchen, returning with a stout pumpkin pie smothered in clouds of whipped cream, and then a mincemeat pie decorated with small curls of orange peel soaked in rum, which she set ablaze just before entering the dining room.

"Why did you get so fancy?" Dad said.

"It's Christmas," Mother responded irritably.

"It's real pretty, Mona," Howard said, while laying a third helping of everything on his plate. But as he finished the remark, his teeth dropped out, clattering onto the table. Nobody spoke; we just stared.

"Well, would you look at that," Howard finally said.

"Ve'd radder not," said Hilma, and Gwen moaned softly.

At that David and I began to howl, and the tension broke. Leon and Elwood smiled.

"Put your teeth back, Howard," Dad said, and we all laughed again. Howard, sobering, chuckled and complied.

"That's the way it is with them boughten teeth," said Leon. "I could never keep 'em in place neither. No sir. They come right out on me all the time. Finally, I just throwed 'em out. Don't need 'em."

"Me neither," said Elwood. "I got strong gooms, real strong. I can near to eat an apple if I had to, with my gooms." He smiled a gummy smile.

The mood quickly shifted from wary and somber, to silly, and David curled his lips over his teeth and tried eating pumpkin pie.

There was ambience now and conversation. Our two guests spoke about former lives when they worked on farms and as lumberjacks. Elwood had been married years before, but had not seen his wife and son in more than twenty years.

"That's awful," said Grandma. "You must miss them."

"Not really. Old lady was a nag. I wasn't good enough for her. She married a bus driver, and I says good riddance. You're better off not getting married in the first place." Then Elwood looked at Grandma. "Ain't every woman good as you, lady."

After dinner we opened presents and there were two packages for the men, who graciously accepted them. Hilma had knitted scarves and wrapped them for our guests, who seemed genuinely touched. About 9:30 Grandma boxed cookies and rolls for the men. We all bade them Merry Christmas and goodbye. Then Dad drove them back downtown.

Christmases over the following years reverted to normal as Grandma's health declined. She was unable to oversee the dinner preparations, which increasingly fell to Mother and Aunt Ada.

But at each of the dinners, conversation invariably drifted to the Christmas when Leon and Elwood visited. Someone always asked if Grandma ever heard from them again, or any of the men she fed. She never did, she said, and never expected to. But that wasn't important. What was important, she always reminded us, was that when you were blessed with plenty, you shared with those who were not.

14

"Yoo-hoo!
It's Me, Olga"

The relationship between Aunt Hilma and Olga Engqvist was an odd one. Though Hilma frequently expressed consternation over Olga's unique behavior, the two retained their friendship more than forty years.

But one mid May afternoon, Aunt Hilma came home from work at Garon's Knitting Mill in West Duluth, fuming as she stomped into the living room. I had just delivered a bag of groceries to Grandma and was about to return home when Hilma arrived, huffing and muttering under her breath. Grandma, who was peeling rutabagas for the evening meal, popped a morsel of raw 'baga into her mouth and looked up at her sister-in-law, who was framed in the doorway. "Why Hilma, what's the matter?" Grandma asked.

Hilma carefully removed her black hat and patted the bun on the back of her head. She continued muttering softly as she took off her black cloth coat and hung it in the entryway. Finally she spoke. "Sometimes, Gustie, I yust vish Olga vould be still and mind her own business. I tell yew, dat voman is plain nuts, if yew ask me."

I chuckled. Hilma complained about Olga's antics at least once a week. Olga's many crotchets often wore on Hilma, who was ever strait-laced and somber. Hilma simply could not abide Olga's playful streak.

There'd been the time several autumns before, when some neighborhood boys were playing a pickup game of touch football, using Grandma's yard for one end zone, and our yard for the other. Hilma had been sitting on her porch, knitting, and Olga, who'd been visiting, became captivated by our game. She made us stop and explain the basics of football to her, and then she asked me to throw her the ball. I gently lateralled it to her and was surprised when she caught it.

"Now, Mickey, do you call that a pass?" she asked.

"Not exactly," I replied. "It was a lateral. You throw a pass overhand." I pantomimed tossing a pass.

Olga turned toward the porch and Hilma, who was frowning at her. "Come on, Hilma," she said. "Run out for a pass. Let's take on the boys."

My friends and I dropped to our knees, collapsed in giggles at the thought of two old ladies flipping a football around. Hilma grunted in disgust and went back into the house. "She's just not a good sport, I guess," Olga said, and threw a perfect spiral back to me.

That was just one of Olga's jocular moments that had needled my great aunt. There'd been many others over the years. And both Grandma and I could sense Hilma was about to expound on yet another.

"Gustie," Hilma started again, straightening her hair, "she can make me so mad." Hilma stepped into the kitchen. "Dere I vas downtown by Fort Awenue. I had yust got off da Grand Awenue bus, and dere vas lots of people around tew. Den all of a sudden, vat do I hear but a real loud vistle. Ewery-body lewked, a course, and den dat Olga, she hewts and hollers, 'Yoo-hoo, Hilma. It's me, Olga.' And she vaves from across da street and comes running to me, and yabbering about da crasy tings she done all day. Vell, I haf to ride home vit her on da bus den tew. And she makes a scene vit da driver about not having no change for tokens. And she laughs and she laughs. Da bus vas crowded tew, and everybody tot she vas nuts. And because she vas vit me, everybody tinks I'm nuts tew."

I laughed, but Hilma shook her head and sat on a kitchen chair. She reached into the pan of sliced rutabaga, extracted a couple of pieces and began gnawing them. "I don't know vy yew tink it's so funny, Mickey. It vasn't yew she made look like a fool. I yust vish she vould keep me out of her goofy notions. I don't like to be seen vit her ven she's vearing Earl's clothes needer."

While I had grown accustomed to Olga's uniqueness, I had not thought her unusual before. But now I was fourteen.

The next week I was downtown myself with a few baseball teammates picking up bats at Tri State Sports on Superior Street. As we walked to the bus stop, we saw Olga come out of Gustafson's Bakery across the street. Though the temperature was in the low seventies, Olga wore her russet winter coat that broke at her ankle. Earl's gray fedora was jammed on her head, fastened down with a plaid wool scarf knotted beneath her chin.

"Hey, look at that looney across the street," said Gary, one of the boys with me.

"She looks like something a hurricane would dump," my other friend, Ray, suggested.

I crimsoned and tried to blend into the crowd on the street so Olga wouldn't see me and embarrass me in front of my friends. We continued walking toward the bus stop, when suddenly I was struck with the idea that Olga too, would be boarding the same bus. "Um, listen you guys," I said. "I think I'm gonna walk home, okay? I don't feel like riding."

Gary and Ray looked at me for a moment. "It's a free country," Ray said. "You wanna hike up them hills, it's your funeral."

Later that afternoon, just before dinner, Mother asked me to take an onion next door to Grandma, who needed one for a recipe. Hilma was already home from work and sat in the living room rocker reading a church magazine. She glanced at me over the tops of her trifocals. "Olga seen yew today," she said. "She vas real disappointed tew."

"Huh? What do you mean?"

Hilma continued rocking, looking at the magazine. "She come over here and said she seen yew and yewr friends downtown and yew didn't vave or nutting."

I thought I detected the trace of a slight smile form on Hilma's lips. "She vas lewking forvard to meeting yewr friends on da bus, but yew vern't on it."

"I walked home," I said. "Needed the exercise."

"Phooey," Hilma said, looking up again. "Yew're yust lucky she did't holler, 'Yoo-hoo, it's me, Olga,' at yew." Hilma gave a pretty decent impression of Olga's soprano warble. "Yew didn't vant to have anyting to do vit her, anymore dan I do dese days. I remember how yew like to laugh ewery time she does someting foolish ven its me she's silly vit. But she'll be silly vit yew yust vunce, and yew'll tink different." Hilma stifled a smirk. "I can't vait," she said, rocking and reading.

About two weeks into summer vacation I joined two friends for a snack at Gustafson's Bakery, after which we were going to take in a matinee movie at the Lyric. Since I sat in the booth facing the rear of the bakery, I didn't see Olga enter and occupy a seat several booths behind us. We were finishing our eclairs and milk when Dick, one of my friends, reached across the table and poked me in the shoulder. "Hey, I think that old lady behind you knows you. She's waving like she wants you to turn around."

I did. "Yoo-hoo, Mickey," Olga called above the din in

the busy restaurant. "You're having a snack downtown, are you?"

My face reddening, I merely nodded and tried to turn back to my friends. "Jeez," I muttered.

"A friend of yours?" Dick said, smirking.

"She lives next door to my grandmother."

I had no sooner gotten the words out of my mouth, when Olga was beside our booth. "Yes, and I've lived in that house for forty-four years. Isn't that something? Forty-four years in the same house. I bet the three of you together aren't forty-four if you add up all your ages."

None of us said anything. "Well, Mickey," she started again, "aren't you going to introduce me to your young friends?"

"Oh, sure, yeah," I said, and managed abrupt introductions of Dick and Dave. Then I told Olga we had to leave so we wouldn't be late for the show.

"Show don't start for another half-hour, Mickey," said Dave, guffawing after we'd gotten outside. Nobody but the family and folks who had known me when I was a young child were permitted to call me Mickey, a name suitable for cute little tuskers, but not for a person who hoped to grow to mature, responsible adulthood. I hated the monicker, and demanded to be called Mike.

Over the next few days whenever Dick and Dave were around, they'd pretend to want me to take them over to Mrs. Engqvist's house to chat and have her tell them stories about me when I was a little kid. I tried changing the subject, but they said if I wouldn't, they'd just go over by themselves sometime when I wasn't around. That thought greatly amused both of them, and they wondered, "What could you tell us about little Mickey, Mrs. Engqvist?" Then they'd both laugh.

One day near the end of July, Aunt Hilma had a doctor's appointment, and Howard was to drive her downtown and back home again. While Hilma got ready to go, Howard spied me pulling the lawnmower from the garage. "Hey, Mickey," he shouted. "You don't want to mow the lawn now, do you?"

"Of course not," I said. "I never want to mow the lawn."

"It'll keep," he said. "Listen, I got to take Auntie down to the sawbones. You come with us, and, while she's having her appointment, we'll go over to Harry Silk's, and I'll teach you to play snooker."

Howard had often talked about playing pool in a pool hall, but I had been forbidden to enter Harry Silk's, because Mother said, "It's a place for idlers and bums, and no kid of mine will hang around idlers and bums." She always cast a stern glance at Howard when she said that in his presence.

But Mother was having her hair fixed at another neighbor's house, and I wanted to learn to play snooker. I especially wanted to get inside a real pool hall, so I left the lawn mower and jumped in the back seat of Howard's Chevy.

Once inside the smokey confines of Silk's upstairs billiard parlor between Second and Third Avenues West on Superior Street, however, I didn't get to play any snooker at all. Some of Howard's cronies were there, and cajoled him into a game of eight-ball. He proceeded to lose nearly ten dollars. Howard was in no mood to teach the game to a green kid, especially after he'd been skinned of his cash in less than half an hour. He didn't speak as we walked back to the Medical Arts Building to pick up Hilma and head home.

Outside it was one of those lush, gorgeous afternoons, with the temperatures hovering in the low eighties, and a southwest breeze carried a lilac ambrosia over the streets. As Howard and I walked along, I felt something strike me in the ankle. I paid no mind, thinking I'd merely been inadvertently kicked by another pedestrian. Several steps further, though, I was struck in a like manner again, and, as I turned, I saw a snowball bounce against Howard's calf. He spun around. We saw no one immediately, but finally from within the throng we heard the all-too-familiar warble, "Yoo-hoo—it's me, Olga," followed by peals of laughter. She caught up to us, laughing so hard tears coursed down her heavily rouged cheeks, mapping them with tiny streams in her makeup. "My, but this is fun," she said. "I certainly surprised you, didn't I? She laughed again. "I should say."

"Snowballs?" said Howard. "In July? Aren't you a little old for these shenanigans, Olga?"

She held up a blue canvas shopping bag. "Here, look," she said, thrusting the bag toward us. It was half-filled with snowballs, and the bag was soaked near the bottom where her weapons had melted through. "You can't imagine the looks on people's faces when they get pelted with a snowball in the middle of summer," she said, laughing some more.

"Where did you get those?" I asked.

"Hah. Remember that snowstorm we had early last May? I'm no fool. I went outside and made me a couple dozen, then kept them in the freezer. I didn't know if they'd last, but they sure did, didn't they? I tell you, I'm having more fun today than a barrel of monkeys."

"I'll tell you what I think, Olga," Howard said sternly. "I think you're coo-coo."

Olga closed the bag and looked over at him. "Well, Howard, if you're not a little bit coo-coo, life certainly would be boring, wouldn't it?" She sobered then and asked if we were going home. When Howard said we were, she prevailed upon him to give her a lift.

"After you pelted me with snowballs?" Howard said.

She offered him the sack. "Oh, all right. Go ahead and throw one at me," she said. "But give me a little head start, okay?" She started a rapid shuffle down the street.

"Oh, for gosh sakes, Olga, I'm just kidding, for crying out loud," Howard said, blushing and handing the snowball sack back to her.

During the drive home Olga kept haranguing Hilma

about snowball fights Hilma may have had during her girl-hood back in Deerwood. Hilma, naturally, would not admit to throwing even one snowball, ever. "Da boys did, yah, but not us girls. Dat vas yust dumb, Olga," Hilma said. "Be-sides, dey're dangerous. Yew could hit somevun in da eyes, and den yew'd haf some trouble."

"The secret is, Hilma," said Olga, "to not aim at a per-son's face. Oh, I tell you, it's a grand feeling to make a nice thick snowball and toss it and have it go *plop* against some-one's fanny." She laughed again.

At the corner of Tenth Avenue East and Ninth Street, Olga leaned forward. "Stop, Howard," she called. "Let me out."

"We're just a block from home," Howard said.

"That's okay," she said excitedly. "There's Jiggs." She pointed to our portly mailman making his rounds. "I want to drill him with a snowball."

Howard pulled over to the curb; Olga exited the car and ran toward Jiggs who was crossing the street in front of Gates' house. "Yoo-hoo, Jiggs," she shouted. "It's me, Olga." Jiggs paused, and Mrs. Engqvist extracted a watery slush ball from her canvas sack. She wound up and threw, missing a direct hit, but the missle splashed on the side-walk in front of Jiggs and sprayed his shoes. He managed a little quick step jump and gave Olga a puzzled stare. Mrs. Engqvist started laughing. She laughed and held her sides. She laughed and sat on the curb. Howard shook his head and started up Tenth Avenue. We could still hear Olga laughing as we pulled into our driveway.

15

April's Fool

During my childhood, Uncle Howard was usually ambivalent about holidays and celebrations. He more or less tolerated them because he was expected to join the family for the festive dinners or picnics. However, he always was edgy and wary whenever All Fool's Day approached. Each April first, from about the time I was eleven or twelve, he stayed in bed all day.

And for good reason. By remaining safely ensconced at home on that day, he might avoid the accumulated vengeance of his victims. Howard, you see, was a man for whom April first, and its attendant highjinks capers, was a year-long endeavor.

The objects of his tomfoolery were ordinary people who held regular jobs—encumbrances outside my uncle's experience. They had neither the time nor the energy Howard had for practical jokes, except on April 1.

Alas, they were rarely successful, though one effort truly needled him. That year, Bert Carlson rounded up several other men, and while Howard cowered under his covers, they laid a coat of pink paint on Howard's front porch. The previous autumn, Howard had painted the house Lincoln green.

As a general rule, though, he was careful to avoid taking on equals, so during my childhood, I was often the butt of his "little tricks," as he used to call them. During a period when he stayed at our house, he'd sometimes call me to the phone to talk to wrong-number callers. Several times he hid all my socks, making me late for school. Once he replaced the hard yellow cheddar in the sandwiches my mother packed in my lunchbox with slices of hard yellow soap. When I was about ten and sick with the flu, Howard called on me in my room one evening. I had to use the bathroom during his visit and when I returned I noticed he had made my bed. Touched by his thoughtfulness, I thanked him. He watched me as I struggled to slide beneath the blankets. He had shortsheeted me.

Yet the tricks he played on me were mild compared to those he foisted on his friends. For instance, an acquaintance of his returned from vacation to find his rural mailbox filled with dead, decaying minnows—a remembrance from Howard. And one winter evening, Bert Carlson rudely awoke five times between midnight and four A.M., to ringing alarm clocks Howard had hidden throughout Bert's bedroom.

In 1947 Ed, an old family friend, visited us at Grandma's house and commented about the quality of pie crusts baked with lard, as opposed to those prepared with shortening. Ed said he much preferred lard. Howard begged to differ. He said lard was rendered pig fat—the same fat Ed's wife would trim from pork chops before frying.

Suddenly a light danced in Howard's eyes. He dashed to the kitchen, returning with containers of lard and shortening. He opened each and brought out a spoon. He dipped it in the lard and asked Ed to examine it for texture and smell. As Ed leaned forward, his mouth opened slightly. Howard popped in the spoon filled with lard. "There, Eddie," he said. "That's the taste of lard for you. Here's the taste of shortening." As poor Ed sputtered and gasped, Howard maneuvered the teaspoon filled with shortening into Ed's mouth as well. The coughing and sputtering continued for several long minutes; all the while Howard argued the superiority of shortening over lard, and he hoped the taste test had convinced Ed too. Ed was one of the men Howard assiduously avoided each April First.

One 1950s Fourth of July, at a large family picnic at my father's summer cottage, Howard said he'd arranged a fireworks display. He urged Dad to invite folks from all around the lake to come and view the show at nine o'clock that evening.

By sundown perhaps seventy-five adults and children gathered on Dad's beach. Some of the kids caterwauled and romped through Dad's new rose garden, prompting him to ask Howard to get the show on the road. Whereupon Howard produced a railroad flare, lighted it, and stuck it in the sand. Facing the crowd, he announced flatly, "Fireworks." Then he got in his car and drove home, leaving my father to attend the increasingly unruly assemblage. Dad was never able to exact an appropriate revenge.

Years did not dim the memory of Howard's "little tricks," and I seemed to have developed a latent instinct for the foolish and absurd myself. Though I long ignored the potential for April Fool's pranks, several seasons back I struck. I rose extra early that morning in preparation. My wife located jello in her shoes, and a bit later that day, my daughters discovered that the hard-boiled eggs they were so fond of taking in their school lunches were not boiled at all.

Epilogue

Christmas Slides

Our family photo album is actually comprised of some dozen volumes dating back to the twenties and thirties, with faded yellowed snapshots of my parents as they looked in their teens and twenties. But the most poignant of the family photographs are not contained in any of the albums, but rather in slides my father began taking in the late 1940s.

Most prominent among them is his collection of Christmas slides, which includes twenty or so shots taken through the mid 1960s. They are not, however, pictures of folks opening packages, or of decorative lighting, or of department store Santas hoisting my younger brothers and me atop the backs of stuffed reindeer.

The slides are of the Fedo-Norquist clan sitting around Grandma Norquist's food-laden table partaking in the annual Christmas Eve feast. They are unremarkable pictures, the kind that would produce bored yawns from anyone outside the family, as there appears to be little difference from one year's slide to the next.

Seating never varied around Grandma's table; Dad at the east end, Howard at the west; and everyone else always assuming his or her position from the previous Christmas dinner.

No one except Dad seemed to enjoy either the picture taking or the viewing of the slides. Dad would wait until everyone, himself included, sat, the food brought to the table and passed around. Then he'd jump up. "Wait—almost forgot the picture."

He'd squeeze around the table to get back to the living room for his Kodak, load it, and then ask us to pose. I think Dad took the slides for his own amusement, just to make everyone wait while plates heaped with holiday comestibles cooled before us.

The rest of us were not pleased. Our faces reflect impatience, indifference, or silliness, yet Dad remained dogged in his determination to capture our family tableau each year. Camera in hand, he adjusted his position, asked someone to move closer to the table, or requested that someone else inch back just a bit.

"Good grief, Mike, just hurry up and take the picture," Uncle Howard would crab. "Stand still and take the picture so we can eat."

Ignoring Howard, whose appetite never seemed to be sated, Dad would say, "Smile at the birdy." Birdy was not one of Dad's words, and he used to wiggle his mustache and roll his eyes to try to arouse mirth.

"Damn the birdy," Uncle Howard muttered in 1950. That picture is distinguished from all the rest because David and I are shown collapsed with giggles, while Hilma, shocked by the epithet, is wide-eyed with mouth agape. Howard's head is in his hands, and his mass of russet hair dominates the lower right-hand corner of the slide.

In other slides, David and I would not smile but jam our mouths with carrot sticks and pose for Dad, cheeks bulging.

Several early 1950s slides show both of us grinning stupidly at spoons mountained with boiled potatoes that we had positioned near our lips. In later shots we have left our clownish, awkward stages and grown into young men with crew cuts, wearing dark suits and exhibiting enigmatic smiles at Dad's ridiculous "birdy."

In every holiday slide at Grandma's the table groaned with traditional Swedish fare: lutefisk, rings of potato sausage, bowls of skinned potatoes, peas, and carrots; rye buns; silver platters with molded jello, cranberries and various relishes.

I remember everything fondly, save the lutefisk, which David and I refused to eat. My Italian father tolerated the quivering mass of lye-soaked cod by inundating it with allspice and ladling on Grandma's white sauce.

Howard, on the other hand, heartily waded in, always slapping hefty portions on his plate. He would slurp the fish and slowly devour platters of food for nearly two hours, chewing slowly, taking bits of bread to mop up sauces, and then wash everything down with strong coffee liberally laced with cream and sugar. Three desserts—pumpkin and mincemeat pies and rice pudding—were *de rigueur* for Howard, and he finished off the meal with several of Grandma's paper-thin ginger Santas.

By the time Howard had gnawed his way to dessert, David and I were beside ourselves with the anticipation of opening our gifts, but we knew we still had to wait until all the dishes were washed and put away before presents could be opened.

Dad grew impatient as well. He preferred to listen to the Bing Crosby Christmas program on our large Philco console, but inevitably had to settle for scratchy snatches of "White Christmas" on Grandma's beige table-model Zenith because of Howard's marathon eating.

Perhaps this was Howard's revenge on Dad for having to pose for the slides year after year.

In the early 1960s, the pictures began to change. Aunt Hilma passed away in 1959, and, viewing the slides now, I'm awash in memories of the wolf tales she used to tell David and me. The 1960 photo is somehow bleak without her stern countenance staring at the camera.

Grandma's death followed in 1961, and Howard's wife, Gwen died the next year. In 1963 I'm not there either, electing to spend the season singing with a folk group at an Omaha coffee house.

The slides were suspended in 1966, when Aunt Ada and Howard came to our house instead of Grandma's, where Ada now lived alone. We no longer consumed lutefisk and potato sausage, but rather prime rib of beef with Yorkshire pudding, or sometimes crown pork roast. Once we had a Dickensian stuffed goose, but none of those viands are captured on film, for Dad seemed to lose his zeal for the Christmas photo after the tradition moved to our house.

Howard, frail and drawn, still mustered an appetite for the occasion, but was as apt to daub his tie in the gravy as his bread. Nobody seemed excited about opening gifts, and our conversations were more sedate without the presence of overstimulated children.

By 1975 I had married and spawned two daughters who seemed to heighten the mood for all of us. After dinner that year, Howard, now lean and crippled, appeared exhilarated. He called to Dad, "Get out your birdy, Mike. Take a birdy."

Dad had forgotten his old key word. "What do you mean, Howard?"

"A picture, Dad," I said. "A slide."

Dad protested weakly. It just wouldn't be the same. Besides, everyone was finished eating. Part of the fun, he said, was in having all the food on the table for the photo.

"Just take the picture," Howard groused.

Dad looked around at the rest of us and said it would take some time. He hadn't used the camera in ages and wasn't sure it would work properly. He spent several minutes loading the Kodak and adjusting his position, as in Christmases past. Howard, smoothing his hair and tightening his tie, demanded, "Everybody smile."

Only Mom, Howard, Ada and my young family are present. David and Stephen were living out of state and could not join us that year. It was the last Christmas Howard and Mother would celebrate. The following year they were ill, and our holiday festivities were somber. They died within three months of each other.

The images on those old slides are precious to me, as is the memory of Dad's Kodak routine. A few years back I took on the role of Christmas photographer, and my technique is reminiscent of Dad's. I putter with aperture, flash, and angles. Dad, in turn, resurrects Howard. "Stop fooling with that camera," he grumbles. "People are hungry and the food's getting cold."

These stories first appeared, in slightly different form, in the following publications:

"Backyard Bear," originally titled, "Wolves, Bears, and Aunt Hilma," *Lake Superior Magazine*, Fall, 1985, Vol. 7, issue 2.
"Christmas Slides," *Minnesota Monthly*, December, 1985, Vol. 19, number 12.

"Christmas, 1953," *Lake Superior Magazine*, Winter, 1985-86, Vol. 8, issue 1.

"Bert Carlson's Winch," *Lake Superior Magazine*, Sept.-Oct., 1986, Vol. 8, issue 4.

"Learning To Spit For Distance," *Lake Superior Magazine*, March-April, 1987, Vol. 9, issue 2.

"Demolition Pike," originally titled, "Demolition Pike of Fish Lake," *Lake Superior Magazine*, November/December, 1987, Vol. 9, issue 6.

"April's Fool," appeared simultaneously in Los Angeles *Herald-Examiner*, and The St. Paul *Pioneer Press*, April 1, 1988.

"Amos Vachter, Actor Extraordinaire," originally titled, "Aunt Hilma and the Villain," *Lake Superior Magazine*, April/May, 1990, Vol. 12, issue 2.

Other Books by North Star Press